VORTEX

DEATH IS SWALLOWED UP IN VICTORY

Harold G. Reynolds

ISBN 978-1-64299-604-3 (paperback)
ISBN 978-1-64299-605-0 (digital)

Christian Faith Publishing, Inc.
832 Park Avenue
Meadville, PA 16335
www.christianfaithpublishing.com

Printed in the United States of America

"Behold, I have set before thee an open door,
and no man can shut it." (Rev. 3:8)

"Death is swallowed up in victory." (1 Cor. 15:54)

"He will swallow up death in victory." (Isa 25:8)

Contents

Author's Disclaimer

VORTEX, DEATH IS SWALLOWED UP in Victory is a warning of Bible prophecy fulfilled about a great prophet Itso, who happens to travel through time and history. The end of Itso's travel through time and history is thus marked by the arrival to the final destination, that being of the temple library. In other words, after all of that travelling around, Itso did settle in the temple library, as also the kingdom of heaven!

A book to be remembered for all eternity, if not for centuries in the future. My intention in the written portrayal of *Vortex, Death Is Swallowed Up in Victory* has been to show this story in a truthful and in a non-fictional manner. The overall theme of "What would you do if you know that you were warned by God that there is going to be a nuclear war?" becomes self-evident as it is mentioned near the beginning of chapter 1. Thereafter does this set the stage for the entire story to unfold itself as it does.

Never in my opinion was the portrayal of *Vortex, Death Is Swallowed Up in Victory* ever, in any way, intended to be too preachy, or dogmatic. I do not regard any one religious organization, cult, or denomination, of which I may have mentioned, to be greater than or lesser than the other. We are all God's children; of which, He does not discriminate among the different individuals or entire nations when it comes to our obedience in our worship of Him.

In the event when sometimes readers do happen to find that *Vortex, Death Is Swallowed Up in Victory* to be as somewhat overwhelming, may I suggest that this is a story taken in the context of its overall theme. This proverbial story about life on a bus, between starting point A and ending point B, is most definitely not for the faint of heart. It is a story about reaching one's destination in life, or in death, regardless of whether or not that destination is on the earth or in the kingdom of heaven!

There is absolutely no intention whatsoever in any way by the author of *Vortex, Death Is Swallowed Up in Victory* to either libel, slander, nor plagiarize the works of any individual or organization. This includes any and/or all the works of a secular and/or of a religious nature.

If you like a story which is truthful, suspenseful, and is stranger than fiction, then this one is the ultimate. It has a theme that sets both the tone and the message, which are then brought about in this book.

A key to the understanding of what *Vortex, Death Is Swallowed Up in Victory* is about would be in further confirmation of that which pertains to The Third Prophecy of Fatima. There is now a revealed, definite timeline that would completely fulfill the third of three 1917 prophecies, which were then given to three Portuguese shepherd children from a vison of the Virgin Mary in the town of Fatima in Portugal.

By use of the main character, whose name happens to be that of Itso, this is a book which deals with intense supernatural and paranormal phenomena. The name Itso is in itself an acronym for a backward spelling of the year 1929. The year of 1929 is key to full understanding of what *Vortex, Death Is Swallowed Up in Victory* is all about.

The year of 1929 would indeed point to the appearance of Hailey's comet, nineteen years earlier, in 1910. The seer Nostradamus's quatrain stating, "the comet shall run" could as well point also to a future comet to fall upon Washington DC that would be the cause of much damage and destruction.

Chapter 1

The Journey

White Robe

Itso had visions. Visions of an angel. Morning visions. Morning visions of the archangel Michael. Of God.

Michael was standing in front of Itso, in a flowing white robe that went down to his feet. No sound did Itso hear of his approaching footsteps, and no observation did Itso make of his feet back then.

Itso had found that his first visions of Michael to be truly terrifying as he did not recognize Michael's actual identity until many years later. Michael's powerful arms were folded, out in front of his chest. Not until also years later did Itso realize that Michael's folded arms would signal a major conflict that was currently then in progress upon the surface of earth.

Michael's flaming eyes and the holy expression on his face had made Itso well aware of the high authority that he is. Another thing that Itso had noticed about Michael was that he had no wings. Bird's wings of the feathered kind, which Itso had viewed in some textbooks, were not present here.

While Michael's eyes gazed directly toward Itso's, he had spoken no word, not even a sound. So startled was Itso by the reality of Michael's presence that Itso had attempted to let forth one loud piercing scream in hopes that Michael would say something, anything. Many attempts later, absolutely no sound would come from Michael or Itso.

What Itso had instantly discovered was that there is no fear in the presence of God. Years later, Itso was to realize exactly just what "no fear" had meant.

Itso's vision of the archangel Michael had suddenly ended as Itso had awoken into the bright morning sunshine. As a boy living in Angus, Ontario, Canada, at the time, it was the late sixties. Now, by the late 1960s, would be about the late spring and early summer solstice of 1967. Around that time, was the Arab-Israeli war conflict in the Middle East.

Happening also, about the same time in 1967, was Itso's parents' large family reunion. It was a family reunion taking place out in the backyard of Itso's parental residence in Angus.

At the reunion, Itso remembered having quite a talk about the subject of death with his older cousin Louise. Itso did remember that he had said something like, "When a person reaches a certain age in their life, is it true they die?"

"Yes, Itso, that is true," was her approximate reply.

Until this point in Itso's life, as a boy of six years, almost seven, Itso had not given the subject of death and dying any serious thought. From that time forward, Itso was a much sadder and a wiser person in the newfound knowledge that Itso was not immortal after all.

Itso had a few astral projections since 1967. Itso's spirit was floating through the universe's dark tunnel and into heaven's rectangular doorway, then back to the earth. Visions Itso had are also of soaring like a bird above the rooftops and above the circle of the earth, with little or no effort. Those out-of-body experiences continued until adolescence. At least, those which Itso could remember.

About seventeen more years would come and go before Itso would see Michael again. Another twenty more years would again come and go after that.

That it was Itso's decision to dedicate his life to Jesus Christ was prompted by the first visions that Itso had of God. March 17, 1971 was the date by which Itso had entered into a New Testament book in writing, of Itso's decision to receive Christ as his personal Savior.

Later that year, in August, Itso had attended a camp for boys called the North Waterloo Everton Camp. There were lots of hiking, games, sports, skits, campfire sing-songs, and arts and crafts, the normal things that go with a camp.

The large wooden dormitory building on its top floor had contained more than enough space for metal-framed, double-decker bunk beds. A huge door had opened up to the balcony walkway outside as it ran the dorm's length behind it. To Itso, it was a building which, in the past, could have been used as a dairy barn with its big wooden posts and beams that supported a high ceiling on the uppermost level.

Located nearby and alongside the dormitory, with a good view from the balcony walkway, was the community swimming pool. Itso had his swimming periods there.

Itso preferred the pool's shallow end, of course. Itso remained thankful to God for chlorinated swimming pools back then. That was the day Itso let go of his own bladder.

One Christmas eve, the local church in Angus had chosen Itso to play in a nativity scene. The part of Joseph really did look fine on the stage. Itso's only guess for it was that there were no speaking parts given for Itso to utter on Joseph's behalf.

Everyone else who had surrounded Itso in that nativity scene on stage were the ones who did all of the talking. The problem was not so much with the players on stage who did their speaking parts very well indeed. It was, however, the audience that was loud. No more plastic glow-in-the-dark Jesus for Itso. Just the real one, thank you very much.

Itso had never forgotten the weekly ukulele classes that he once had taken at public school. You know the one. The instrument that looks like a mini guitar but had only a total of four strings.

To this day, Itso thought, no, Itso could have sworn that he had played every song on the ukulele off-key. Itso knew that he did. How many times Itso had practiced at home did not really seem to matter much.

Itso's three favorite songs that were played in class back then were "Raindrops Keep Falling on My Head" by B.J. Thomas, "Put Your Hand in the Hand" by Anne Murray, and "Four Strong Winds" by Ian Tyson.

Who could ever forget the "Four Strong Winds" song that was played by Ian Tyson at the memorial for the four slain Royal Canadian

Mounted Police officers from Alberta in early 2005. Significant it is for Itso that one of the slain RCMP officers should be from the community of Whitecourt Alberta.

As it happened, it did not matter much how often that Itso had played the ukulele. Those relentless schoolyard bullies were already taunting the words, "Itso's got a girlfriend," over and over again like some Gregorian monks in a monastery meal chant. Perception anywhere near the reality would tell Itso that he was indeed their next "monkey meal," or target, having had a broken ukulele and therefore nothing available to sing with. So much for ukuleles. So much for nuclear war.

While some obvious despair that had set in by this time, Itso had nevertheless remained a great believer in godly providence. They did not know though, for Itso could not tell them of his first visions of God.

Questions on the Bus

Now there is "a riddle wrapped inside a mystery, inside an enigma" as Itso had somewhat quoted in a Churchillian manner, pertaining to Russia, which begs to be answered in Itso's life thereafter: "What would you do if you knew that you had been warned by God that there is going to be a nuclear war?"

A ninety-nine-dollar bus ticket, the elders of a small chapel in central Ontario had given Itso, was supposed to be the trip of a lifetime. At least from the point of view of a young and ambitious twenty-three year-old in the spring of 1984.

After all, what better way to obtain some volunteer work experience and stay away from trouble? Or so it was thought of at that time. Little could Itso have imagined in his wildest of dreams as to what extent that Itso's trip to Alberta, Canada, would forever become the life-altering event that it actually did turn out to be.

Major bus-terminal cities listed on the ticket included Sudbury, Ontario; Winnipeg Manitoba; and Edmonton, Alberta. Next, it was on to Grande Prairie, Alberta, and then on to Spirit River further to the north of Alberta.

When Itso's bus arrived north at the Sudbury terminal from Barrie by late evening, the sky had turned to night, and it had started to snow.

Waiting inside the bus station awhile, Itso eventually had proceeded to the connecting bus which travelled from Sudbury to Winnipeg. It had taken about two days' travel, when all of the smaller stops in-between were completed, for the bus to finally reach the city of Winnipeg.

During the Sudbury to Winnipeg trip portion, there were endless hours of evergreen trees just whizzing right past Itso as he sat in the bus seat next to the window. Fortunately, Itso had in his possession an end-times paperback book entitled, *The Rapture: Truth or Consequences*, by author Hal Lindsey. It was to keep Itso himself company in the event that the scenery outside would become a bore. After a while had passed, the tree scenery did become a bore.

God's heavenly providence, however, must have been at work by the next day. On that morning, Itso did not eat anything at all. It was now the afternoon, and Itso was still on the way to Winning, that a sweet, middle-aged-looking woman had given Itso a sandwich to eat.

Out of nowhere did she quite suddenly appear. There was no time for Itso to be startled by what was happening. Much appreciated though was the sandwich which Itso had gratefully accepted from her.

To this day, Itso had wondered, *How did she know that I was hungry and in need of some nourishment, having not let anyone know of my own immediate condition?*

Itso was just about ready to ask this new stranger as to how she knew that he was hungry, but by the time that Itso had finished the sandwich, she was gone. Thereafter did Itso make a decision to be careful and not let himself go hungry again in future.

Winnipeg Terminal

AT THE HUGE WINNIPEG TERMINAL in the late evening dusk, the bus had finally arrived. It would be hours before Itso could catch the connecting bus to Edmonton via Calgary, so Itso had put away his heavy, four black-castor-wheeled brown suitcase into an unoccupied locker.

Just before it had closed for the night, Itso grabbed something to eat from the terminal cafeteria. Packaged goods and fresh aromas there in the display cases would similarly come back to Itso many years later because those food items are also displayed in the Temple Public Library Café.

When Itso had finished eating, he tried to phone an old friend of his, James, whom he had not seen in the many years since he had moved to Winnipeg from Angus, Ontario. By then, it was now very late in the evening, and Itso's attempt to use more than one of the bus station payphones had proven to be unsuccessful.

Either the phones were out of order, or the number that Itso had dialed was not in service. Never did Itso get to see his old friend James though. Maybe someday he will. Later on, when the journey toward Spirit River would soon be complete would there be another, and an even older, friend waiting to meet Itso again.

Itso's next decision was either to check in to a Winnipeg hotel room for the rest of the night or to nap out the hours which had remained for the connecting bus to arrive at the station's waiting area. It had seemed okay for Itso at that time to choose the nap-out option as he had no money for a hotel room of any kind.

Itso did manage to have some breakfast early the next morning shortly after the cafeteria had opened. Soon thereafter, the bus to

Edmonton by way of Calgary had arrived. With Itso's big brown leather suitcase now vacated from the yellow bus-terminal locker, Itso had patiently waited in line at the platform to board.

Itso did wait, that is, until a rough and rude baggage handler, shouting unprintable obscenities, yanked Itso's large suitcase right out of his hand. He then slammed the suitcase into the luggage space beneath the passenger deck. Itso did smell no alcohol on the baggage handler whatsoever.

Itso's first guess was he must be having some sort of a bad, stress day, and therefore had decided to rant and rave away on someone. Someone like me should be such a fortunate target of that.

Itso's second guess was not everyone approves of people napping-out overnight at bus terminals, waiting for the night-shift bus to arrive. Must have been the night shift.

To Itso's immense relief, another angel or bus passenger had quickly came to Itso's rescue, verbally putting the baggage handler in his place. Never did Itso see that strange male helper coming toward Itso, nor did Itso see that confrontational luggage handler again either before, or since that time.

Stops In-Between

From Winnipeg to Calgary, Itso's bus trip had included all of the stops in-between, and it had taken about two days' journey to complete. As the bus did travel down the TransCanada highway, past endless miles of flat prairie wheat fields, Itso could faintly begin to notice the vast and huge expanse of the North American continent. This was an observation which came for someone like Itso who was so used to the environment of urban Ontario.

During the day, Itso had already taken in his fair share of prairie, small-town bus stops, and old timber-planked grain elevators. The local people were continuously boarding and exiting the bus, going on their way to their usual places of employment.

A day of bus travel had now passed by from the time that the bus had departed from Winnipeg. Endless acres of wheat fields had continued to pass by Itso's window as night time was fast approaching. There was no one sitting in the aisle seat beside Itso now. It was time for Itso to settle down and sleep for the night, having already reached to turn off the reading lamp above him.

Itso's end-time rapture book now put away, Itso propped his head up against the bus wall beneath the window. Itso's legs and feet laid across the other empty seat beside him. Itso's feet had now faced the center aisle of the bus.

Outside was the moon casting its soft, glowing, and shimmering light up in the clear sky. There was not much of anything else to see outside of the window as the bus did continue its travel on into the night.

Itso must have slept well through the entire night and into part of the next morning because before Itso had known what happened,

Itso's bus had crossed the provincial border, from Saskatchewan into Alberta. When Itso had reflected back upon this point in his trip, he could only have assumed that it was the holy angels who had wanted to see that Itso was very well rested. It would definitely be in consideration of who Itso would be later meeting with in Alberta.

Itso marveled at the modern Calgary skyline and those lofty foothills in the background as Itso's bus entered the city. Itso's bus then arrived into the terminal.

On the next bus that travelled the provincial highway between Calgary and Edmonton, the numerous cattle ranches and oil wells had become all too evident. Already departed from the Calgary station by late morning, Itso's bus had finally arrived in Edmonton by early evening.

Another Angel?

CHURCH ELDERS EXPECTING ITSO'S ARRIVAL by bus to Edmonton were there to greet Itso. Very grateful was Itso for their kind hospitality when Itso had stayed there overnight in their home. Late the next morning, Itso had boarded the bus again for the trip to continue its travel of the entire distance from Edmonton to Grande Prairie.

Shortly after Itso had departed Edmonton, once again, he opened *The Rapture* book that was with him. It was a book bought earlier at a second-hand thrift store back in Barrie, Ontario. Itso resumed reading from where he had bookmarked.

Suddenly sitting beside Itso in the aisle seat was a male of approximately late teens or early twenties in age. He seemed to be listening to some music by means of a portable radio and earphones. Music listening was something that Itso did not mind to do himself, although Itso had no radio with him at this time.

The male person appeared to be of Asian descent, with straight black hair, cut short, and dark yellow skin. Itso did not get to say anything to him and vice versa.

Itso had thought it very peculiar, however, that he had continued to smile during the entire time that he had sat beside Itso. After a while had passed, Itso began to wonder whether all of that smiling was because of the music that he was listening to or whether it was because of the rapture book that Itso possessed. Before Itso could even think the next thought, he was gone as quickly as he came.

Again, Itso had to wonder later, when he had reflected back on this point in time. *Was there something that he knew, something that*

I did not know? Was he yet another holy angel that was sent by God for observation purposes?

Itso did remember the nice angel lady with the sandwich near the beginning of his trip. Itso did also remember the Good Samaritan bus-passenger angel that put the rude baggage handler in his place back in Winnipeg.

Do these three angelic events in some way point to the three angels' messages that are found in Revelation chapter fourteen in the Bible? thought Itso.

Most of all, did Itso remember the secondhand rapture book that he had taken along for the entire length of the Spirit River retreat trip and back? For it was this very book entitled, *The Rapture: Truth or Consequences*, by author Hal Lindsey through which God had allowed His blessings to follow with Itso.

The aisle seat beside Itso was now empty. It was not to remain empty for much longer.

Windbreaker Blue

WHEN ITSO'S BUS HAD REACHED the stop at Whitecourt Alberta, that was when it happened—Itso's second vision-encounter with God. Itso distinctly had heard the driver open the front door of the bus, which had prompted Itso to glance up from his book. A new passenger had emerged. He had no wings of the feathered kind that Itso could see as before.

Although Itso had said nothing orally at this point, it was instant recognition from here on in, the same being that Itso saw years ago, having first visions of him in Angus as a boy. He was not wearing a white robe this time.

On his very strong and bulky frame, he wore a sky-blue windbreaker type of a jacket and dark navy blue trousers. Very appropriately attired he was for the cool spring weather of May. Unmistakably confident were the sound of his approaching footsteps. He approached the empty seat beside Itso, and in it, he sat down.

"What is your name?" Itso asked.

"Michael," he replied.

"Are you a Christian?"

"Yes."

"So am I."

Imagine, if you will, how, that if Michael were Jesus the Christ, then he would have simply acknowledged this fact in an instant with a statement such as "I am who I am," or "I am He." Instead, we have a simple "Yes."

This, therefore, had led Itso to believe that the archangel Michael, as the personification of the Holy Spirit and His Son

Jesus Christ, are two separately distinct physical beings. They are also recognizable to each other as being in possession of the same Holy Spirit.

"Do you have a girlfriend?" Itso asked.

"I had a girlfriend once, but I broke up with her," Michael said.

Now at this point in the conversation, Itso had to wonder, *The archangel Michael has a girlfriend? How can that be?*

Years later, when Itso was baptized into the Mormon church, Itso had made the connection between Adam of the book of Genesis and the archangel Michael of the book of Revelation in the Bible. Itso had concluded that they are one and the same person here.

It had never occurred to Itso back in the spring of 1984 to ask Michael whether or not the name of his girlfriend that he "broke-up" with was Eve. Even so many years later, when Itso had his third vision-encounter of the archangel Michael at the Temple Public Library Café in June of 2004, Itso had still hoped to ask Michael that very question about Eve in the future.

"Don't Give Me That"

"Do you have a job?" Itso asked.

"Yes," Michael replied.

"What kind of a job do you have?"

"I work with emotionally disturbed children."

"I guess I'm emotionally disturbed too!"

"Don't give me that!"

How, with such authority and effectiveness, did Michael use those words of his rebuke toward Itso! So thunderstruck was Itso at Michael's rebuke of his "I guess I'm emotionally disturbed too!" comment, by Michael's "Don't give me that!"

What must Itso have been thinking? This pointless trip to nowhere? On the bus? The rapture bus?

It was like Michael knew who he was to rebuke Itso. Like Michael knew who Itso was as a Christian. Like Michael was certainly watching Itso for a long time, like those first white-robed visions Itso had in Angus.

A long pause had thus ensued after Michael's rebuke of Itso. Then suddenly, Michael said, "I'll let you read your storybook," as he vacated the aisle seat beside Itso.

"Storybook!" Itso gasped to himself.

"However on earth can such a seriously heavy subject on the rapture be dismissed of as just merely a storybook? Second-hand bookstore paperbacks notwithstanding!"

Upon a deeper analysis of the situation, however, something had soon occurred to Itso. *Oh, yes, of course*, Itso thought. As the main subject of *The Rapture*, the book that Michael had noticed in

Itso's hand, would have merely been like a grade one, primary school read to him.

Having now read awhile, Itso glanced up from his book to see that Michael had moved to the empty row of seats at the front of the bus. Michael was not sitting upright in one of the seats as Itso would have normally expected.

As Michael had stretched across the two front-row seats, as if he were lying on top of a bed, Itso could not help but to be struck by Michael's obvious humility. Michael lay there, in much the same position that Itso had laid earlier on in the trip, when the previous bus had travelled quietly overnight, non-stop throughout most of Saskatchewan.

The only difference was that Michael's head was in the aisle seat while his feet were up beneath the window. Michael was not facing Itso. Itso only saw Michael's backside with the seats lowered. Itso had guessed that Michael was likely talking to the bus driver who was in the nearby driver's seat across from the sliding doors.

Itso did return back to his reading. When the bus had reached the next stop at Valleyview, Itso had glanced up once more and looked out of the window. Outside, in front of the depot, stood Michael with his sky-blue windbreaker talking cordially with the uniformed bus driver as if they knew each other very well. As Itso was obviously out of earshot, Itso could only see their lips moving.

Itso could now see that there was a light, misty spring drizzle falling outside. The very young and newly green leaves on the deciduous trees were still sprouting.

Having seemingly lost all sense of natural timing, Itso turned his glance away from the bus window. Finishing a bottle of soda, Michael was once again sitting beside Itso just as the bus's engine had started back up again.

Watching Over Me

"Do you go to school?" Itso asked.

"Yes," Michael replied.

"What school do you go to?"

"I go to school in Grande Prairie."

Now from God's point of view, or Itso's own interpretation of his point of view, "Do you go to school?" meant, "Are you watching over me?" His reply was yes, in any case.

"What school do you go to?" meant, "Where are you watching over me?" And "I go to school in Grande Prairie," meant, "I am watching over you, in Grande Prairie."

Only one thing had remained for Itso to conclude with any discernment at all. It was that Michael knew that Itso was going to get off the bus at Grande Prairie no matter what!

"Can I live where you are living?" asked Itso.

"No," was Michael's reply.

Now why would Itso ask Michael that question? "Can I live where you are living?"? It was because Itso had what he thought was little or no reason for going to that spiritual retreat located just outside the community of Spirit River, Alberta. A feeling that the entire point of going there was a complete waste of time could no longer be denied upon Itso's part. That Itso probably would have lasted not more than about two weeks at the retreat was nothing more than a testimony to that idea.

Some people may like to call that kind of attitude nothing more than a typical twenty-three-year-old angst, but that is exactly what did happen, as in the length of time whereby Itso did actually stay at the retreat!

Any other place, Itso had thought, would have been a better option. That better option had, in Itso's mind, included the place where God so happens to be living!

This is the reason why Itso believed that Michael had said no. Well, when Itso had looked back to that time in 1984, Itso had guessed that it was because God knew that there were other missions for Itso to accomplish here on this earth. Itso's mortal frame would not have had the proper preparation enough to be able to enter the Kingdom of Heaven until all of Itso's missions were therefore completed on earth. When Michael had said no, a pause had thus ensued, and Itso had questioned Michael no further about this.

The Witness Book

ANOTHER QUESTION DID COME TO Itso, and it had pertained to the real identity of Michael. Without any prompting on Itso's part, Michael had suddenly said, "I was born on the second of August, 1950."

Now, there was only one thing which Itso could understand about this statement from God the Father at that time. Between the time of August 2, 1950, and May of 1984, would thus have Michael with the biological age of thirty-three years and nine-months. This would be, in Itso's estimation, roughly the same age as Jesus Christ when he was thus crucified on the cross.

Was Michael trying to tell Itso that he was Jesus Christ? The answer to this question, in Itso's opinion, was a definite no. Surely, it cannot be denied though that God certainly does know exactly how to focus upon Itso's attention!

The answer to this quite puzzling birthday question was finally revealed to Itso, on January 16, 2001. Itso had observed on a historical events wall calendar at a Kingdom Hall meeting of Jehovah's Witnesses. The date August 2, 1950, had suddenly jumped out at Itso like a huge, brilliant shock of lightning! Quite a gasp had been uttered from Itso's lungs.

On this leap of faith, such a tremendous one at that, did Itso make the name connection between the archangel Michael and Jehovah God as the being of one and the same person! Here was one answer to that mystery date.

The entire work of the Jehovah's Witnesses', *New World Translation* of the Holy Scriptures, was originally released in six volumes from the year 1950 to 1960. The first of those volumes was published to the world on the exact date of August 2, 1950.

A revised complete edition of the *New World Translation* appeared in 1961. Other revisions have followed since that first complete edition of 1961.

The 1984 revision that Itso have includes a forward page, which outlines a brief general history. At the bottom of this page, the last line, is dated June 1, 1984. When Itso was talking to Michael back in May of 1984, Itso did not know that this book was even yet to come into existence!

Substituted by the word *Lord* or *God* in other previous versions of the Bible over the centuries, the word *Jehovah* had almost completely disappeared. Only on August 2, 1950, did the word *Jehovah* begin to be completely restored again with the *New World Translation.*

This restoration of the word *Jehovah* was one reason why Michael had said to Itso that he was born on August 2, 1950. The other reason for this birthday, as Itso was to discover years later, has to do with the biblical generation cycle which lasts for seventy years!

A Test of Numbers

WHEN AFTER A SHORT WHILE had passed, Michael then administered to Itso a test. Michael's soda bottle has now been emptied of its contents. Michael thus revealed to Itso two small and different packages of food, both of which were wrapped with a plastic type of packaging. These were a reminder to Itso of the snack packs regularly sold in cafeterias and cafés.

On the first packet was the name Saloon Nuts in red lettering. Like the soda pop bottle before it, a few moments later, Michael made the packaging of Saloon Nuts disappear as if a magician. Then Michael brought about the packet on which was the name Pitted Sunflower Seeds. This second pack was in yellow lettering.

Before Itso had realized what was actually taking place here, Itso's arms had suddenly bolted out in front of him as if he were sleepwalking. The only difference was that Itso was wide awake and sitting down. Both of Itso's two hands were now cupped together as if he were in some sort of a dream.

Out of the now opened bag of Pitted Sunflower Seeds had Michael proceeded to pour much of its contents into Itso's two hands. When Michael had finished pouring, Itso did eat up all of the sunflower seeds that were in Itso's hands.

This was a strong reminder to Itso of the entire sandwich, which he had eaten earlier, provided by the nice angelic lady back when he had travelled on his way to Winnipeg. Thus, God's blessing upon Itso was now assured, with Itso having now passed this test in so many ways!

There is, however, a much deeper meaning to those two packages going on here. The twenty letters of the yellow Pitted Sunflower

Seeds package do look and sound so much better than the ten letters of the red Saloon Nuts package. This is what Itso had discovered.

Why would the yellow color be the dominant one instead of red? Itso wondered.

Soon after, it became quite obvious to Itso that the yellow represents the endless glory of God's undefiled priesthood in heaven. The color red represents the very destructive nature of Satan and of his priesthood on earth!

Twenty letters on the yellow package versus ten letters on the red one. Itso had further discovered that this alludes to the fact that in accordance with the book of Revelation 12:4 in the Bible, there are twenty of God's holy angels for every ten fallen ones.

Talking about big things coming in small packages is not just a common cliché to Itso. Itso did see those packages, and he does know the words which are on them!

Itso had found other sets of interesting facts also that were evident upon closer examination. Itso had removed four vowels from Saloon Nuts and then the seven vowels out of Pitted Sunflower Seeds. The resulting number added together is eleven. In wake of the September 11, 2001, tragedy, Itso had discovered from media sources that eleven is the ancient Babylonian number for banking and commerce. Itso did conclude one thing from number eleven.

Could this be then what Michael had meant when he said, "I work with emotionally disturbed children" upon Itso asking him earlier what kind of a job he had?

Of course though, Itso naturally did not like any idea of overplaying the numbers game or of speculation, or of reading into things that are simply not there. That being said, however, Itso did make an interesting comparison between the ten letters of Saloon Nuts, and the ten Bible commandments from the book of Exodus 20:3–17.

In Itso's opinion, the four vowels in Saloon Nuts could easily allude to the first four commandments which pertain directly to God. This is in accordance to the book of Exodus 20:1–11 in the King James Version of the Bible.

There's that number eleven again! thought Itso.

Many more years were to pass by before Itso was to make another significant discovery in 2013. When Itso had juxtapositioned the five words—saloon nuts, pitted sunflower seeds–together, he had received some interesting results.

With the exception of *pitted*, the other four words do consist of the letter *s*. Only one of the words actually contains two *s*'s. The number of *s*'s therefore totals five in number altogether.

What Itso had discovered about the letter *s* is that as the nineteenth letter of the alphabet, it is repeated among the four words a total of five times for a sum of ninety five in number. Itso next had then applied this very sum to a nineteen-year political cycle of ninety-five years. Itso had also noticed that all of the other letters between the five *s*'s had also totaled nineteen in number!

The only word with no *s*, Pitted, was not therefore part of the other nineteen letters. Itso had also discovered that every individual letter in the word *pitted* could be discerned with an ominous message which has six words—"Pentagon in tidal tsunami earthquake destruction."

Itso had also discovered that the ominous six-word earthquake message did not end with only six words formed from the one *pitted* word. Itso was thereafter able to form an expanded message with the nineteen other letters that had remained from the five dropped *s* letters from the other four words.

The newly expanded message now looked like it had consisted of twenty-five letters when Itso had listed those five words together with the five *s* letters now dropped. The message now looked like this—"aloon nut, itted unflower eed."

What on earth was Itso to even make of this strange combination of letters? As Itso continued to study and to pray, an answer was soon to come in three general points:

- "aloon nut" points to the rule of antichrist;
- "pitted" points to the already mentioned "Pentagon in tidal tsunami earthquake destruction, and;
- "unflower eed" points to the words: United Nations (building) found, lower earthquake damage.

What, then, was Itso to understand from these three general points? To Itso, all three points to him had sounded like they were newspaper headlines!

Itso had considered the fact that vowels such as *a, o, o,* and *u* in Saloon Nuts can also be rendered to mean four words that describe exactly who God really is. Words such as *almighty, omnipotent, omnipresent,* and *universal.* These are just a few examples which describe who God is from Itso's point of view. There do abound further examples which describe God's identity.

Itso had also seriously considered the fact that the number seven is generally agreed to be God's universal number. It is a number which stands for the completeness of God's creation as indicated in the Bible books such as Genesis, Daniel, and Revelation. Itso did have reason to believe in the completeness of God's creation as he had continued to look into more about the number seven.

"Got to Go to Sleep Now"

OUTSIDE, THE SKY HAD TURNED completely dark by the time that Itso's bus had arrived into the Grande Prairie terminal. Waiting there in anticipation for Itso's exit from off the vehicle at any moment were a few of the younger people from the retreat, which was located just outside of the Spirit River community. They had driven their pickup truck all of the way from there in order that it was possible for them to meet Itso at the terminal.

Moments before Itso was to exit from his window seat, Itso's friend Michael had then uttered what was to later be both some very comforting and some very chilling words. Only once, did Michael repeat these same words, "Got to go to sleep now; Got to go to sleep now."

Much like Michael's earlier statement of "Don't give me that," Itso was completely awestruck. Having had read through most of *The Rapture* book and some biblical verses by that time, Itso had instantly recognized then that the Christian word for sleep meant death! (John.11:11–14)

When Itso reflected back on this once-repeated statement from Michael, he found it true that Michael was indeed talking about death to come. The only thing was that the death which was mentioned here by Michael would not happen until it was many years later.

What Itso's young twenty-three-year-old brain would only conclude back then in 1984 was that Itso had merely two more years to live! Michael, for as he earlier had turned down Itso's brilliant idea of living immediately with him in the Kingdom, had allowed Itso's feelings to naturally not be in a very good mood for the next two years.

Notwithstanding all of that though, Itso had managed to acquire a maintenance job at camp Glen Mhor, Muskoka, Ontario, for the next few summers of 1984 and 1985. Mostly of down-to-earth work, the maintenance job, involved to keep clean all the flush toilets and to have all of the outhouses limed at the camp.

Itso had found that much like the North Waterloo Everton camp, there were swimming, hiking, games, sports, play-acting, campfire sing-songs, and arts and crafts, the normal things which constitute a camp. Itso had then thought, *This time, and thank God, there were no problems with my bladder.*

When the two-year period of time for which Itso thought that he should have been dead had expired, Itso did remain unexpired and still very much around. Now was the time for Itso to look more closely at what "Got to go to sleep now," once repeated, had really meant. In later years, Itso had discovered that it too had read like a newspaper headline.

By April of 1987, Itso was working in the mailroom. Itso's job there was to insert ad fliers for a local Barrie newspaper. Itso did not think much about newspaper headlines or coded messages back then. It had to be the providence of God that had Itso in the mailroom.

From 1991 to 1993, Itso had completed a few Bible prophecy courses through the local Seventh-Day Adventist church. The providence of God was now to begin to work its miracles in Itso's life. (See *God Cares: Volume One* for Daniel, and *God Cares: Volume Two* for Revelation in the Bibliography.)

Chapter 2

The Church

Five Loaves and Two Witnesses

Itso had discovered that as the name Seventh-day Adventist implies, the important thing about them is that they so do happen to worship God every Sabbath-Day Saturday, the seventh and last day of the seven-day weekly cycle. This is in contrast to most church denominations today who obviously worship God on Sunday, the first day of each week. The prophecy courses, which Itso had completed, do go quite extensively into the history of how the worship of God at church each week was gradually changed from Saturday to the present Sunday.

Another thing that Itso had discovered about the SeventhDay Adventist is that they are also great believers in "the three angels' messages." These three messages are described in Revelation chapter 14 of the Bible.

Itso truly believes that to understand and appreciate a full meaning of the three messages is to understand and appreciate the full objective of the seven letters to the seven churches. These seven letters had plainly unfolded themselves as they are read in Revelation chapters 2 and 3.

Itso also believes that each of the seven churches on the earth is named in accordance to their timespan, from the day of earth's creation until all of the way to the second coming of Christ. Seven church names, in both concurrent and consecutive order, are Ephesus, Smyrna, Pergamum, Thyatira, Sardis, Philadelphia, and Laodicea.

Two of the seven churches, Itso believes, of which God through Jesus Christ does not criticize, are the two suffering churches of Smyrna, or "the resurrection," and Philadelphia, or "the rapture."

Itso's emphasis upon both of these two churches is reasonable because they are in direct contrast with the other five churches who have both good and evil things about them. Five churches perfectly reflect the tree of the knowledge of good and evil in Eden, while the other two humble churches are the result which springs from the Tree of Life in Eden.

Itso could easily see how, therefore, in chapter 3, verse 7 of Revelation that the churches of Smyrna, or "resurrection," and Philadelphia, or "rapture," are linked. Both are identified as thus the two witnesses of Revelation 11:3!

In the following paragraph, Itso has provided his own interpretation of Revelation 3:7.

"He that openeth, and no man shutteth, is Philadelphia, or rapture; And shutteth, and no man openeth, is the Smyrna door of 'death into paradise,' or the first death."

The Smyrna door of death and paradise, Itso believes, is also of the resurrection from paradise and mortality into the kingdom of heaven at the start of the great tribulation! In verse eight of Revelation chapter 3, the church of Philadelphia, or rapture, is further identified as "an open door and no man can shut it"; or in other words, no man can prevent this event to take place at a certain point in time.

Itso believes that the open and closed door also refer to the persecution on earth of some of God's saints. This is a persecution which does occur when paradise itself has been suddenly eliminated at the beginning of the three-and-a-half-year great tribulation. This is a great tribulation that is consequential to the Smyrna church's resurrection from paradise into heaven.

The repentant saints of God, who remain behind, will now go directly into heaven as a result of the great time of the testing, or of tribulation, upon the earth. From now on, the reward of these repentant saints instantly go with them as is mentioned in Revelation 14:13.

Itso had noticed that in this, the Philadelphia church is situated before the Smyrna church and is greatly symbolic as the Lord's Supper arrangement of 1 Corinthians 11:24–26. Here, we have the breaking of the bread first of Philadelphia, and then the drinking of the cup last of Smyrna. What this would then say to Itso is that the rapture of the first part of the church will actually occur before the resurrection of the second part of the church.

Itso had also discovered that for any wedding to properly take place at a church, all of the guests would have to be notified, dressed properly, arrived, and seated ahead of time. The point of the wedding here is that while all Smyrnans are Philadelphians, but not all Philadelphians are Smyrnans! It was now that Itso had pondered the question: "Will this proper dressing of the rapture church of Philadelphia happen shortly before the arrival of the bride church of resurrected Smyrna?"

Itso had continued to read 1 Thessalonians 4:13–18 in the Bible very carefully. Itso had also read 1 Corinthians 15:51–58.

Itso had remembered now, from when he had earlier before mentioned in chapter 1, about his spirit floating through the universe's dark tunnel into heaven's rectangular doorway, and then back to earth again in truth. The lighted, rectangular doorway that Itso had observed spinning and twirling like a baton in a parade, had remained stationary. It was, thus, Itso himself who was spinning through the dark tunnel. Itso could only venture to guess at this point in time what that doorway was to represent. *Was this a doorway into and out of a spaceship, or the Kingdom of Heaven itself?*

Itso could now see that there really is a huge difference between the Kingdom of Paradise and the Kingdom of Heaven. In an age before the second advent of Jesus Christ, paradise is therefore the place where all spirits go, who have separated from their bodies upon death. Paradise itself can be further defined as a kingdom of mortal spirits, but not of immortals and those who are destined to be resurrected as immortal spirits. Itso believes that this event will come to pass when Jesus Christ does return again to take and to unite his bride, the church of Smyrna, at the resurrection wedding!

Only the Kingdom of Heaven, Itso believes, can be properly defined as the place where immortal spirits can dwell. It is the first and the original existent state of holy angels. Here is where Itso believes that there is absolutely no difference between the body and the spirit which does possess it. One is just a mere extension of the other, united in one, and is therefore united with God.

Itso also believes that the abyss, or Hades, on the other hand, is diabolically the opposite of paradise. It is the kingdom of spirits for those souls whose dead bodies now separate from them, will be along with their spirits, eventually thrown into what is called the lake of fire. The lake of fire, therefore, means the ultimate destruction of both body and soul, or spirit, forever from the sight and presence of God in the Kingdom of Heaven.

To further support that which Itso has discovered is to read the New Testament book of John 3:16. It is a verse that says in the King James Version, "For God so loved the world, that he gave his only begotten Son, that whosoever believeth in him should not perish, but have everlasting life."

Itso has also considered the possibility that in Revelation 3:7, where it says, "He that openeth, and shutteth, and no man openeth," could also point to the two doors of the summer and winter solstices mentioned in Matthew 24 of the holy Bible. The ten virgins of Matthew 25, who are of church history in Revelation, all do fit quite nicely with both summer and winter solstices. This is because Itso does believe that it is the five wise virgins who get to go to the wedding feast of eternal life while it is the foolish ones who are prevented from entering the feast due to their wasted opportunity of not preparing for it!

Diasporas One and Two

ITSO HAD NEXT TURNED TO the Bible book of Daniel 9:2. Here, Itso had read that the prophet Daniel was understanding "by books the number of years, whereof the Lord came to Jeremiah the prophet, that he would accomplish seventy years in the desolations of Jerusalem."

Itso had carefully noted that the term "desolations" is plural, and is not in the singular term of "desolation." This, therefore, did indicate to Itso that the true church on earth, as symbolized by Jerusalem, was to undergo more than one period of persecution on the earth, that of which is to last for seventy years reach in length.

Diaspora one was the seventy-year captivity to Babylon of Juda, a tribe from Jerusalem. This captivity was from 604–534 years before the birth of Christ.

Itso had learned that the prophet Daniel was a Jewish upper-class family member of Jerusalem's royal household before his captivity to Babylon in his teens. Daniel was one, who by God's grace could actually tell king Nebuchadnezzar of Babylon about the meaning of a dream that concerned the future and which had troubled the king in his sleep. It was a dream about a future which had extended to our day. Itso also believed that other prophets, like Isaiah, Jeremiah, and Ezekiel, may well have helped influence Daniel to follow God's love when as a boy in Jerusalem.

In the Church of Latter-Day Saint's Book of Mormon, in the third book of Nephi chapter 8 is given what Itso believes to be the actual crucifixion date of our Lord and Savior Jesus Christ. The fifth verse has stated, "In the thirty and fourth year, in the first month, on the fourth day of the month."

Itso's interpretation of this time, therefore, is January fourth, thirty-four years after the birth of Christ! In Itso's opinion, there was obviously quite a lot of shaking going on in the worldwide environment at that time! The time of the actual crucifixion is a date for which other church denominations may most certainly disagree.

Itso had now some questions of his own concerning the crucifixion of Christ and beyond:

1) Did the crucifixion of Christ in 34 AD mark the beginning seventy years persecution of the Christians during the church age of Smyrna-Resurrect?

2) Had this persecution continued until, say 104 AD, when the church apostasy was firmly established by then?

3) Was it not, after all, in 70 AD that the second Jewish temple in Jerusalem, rebuilt from the first one shortly after the first "diaspora" in Babylon, was to be mostly destroyed by the Roman army?

4) Was it not at roughly the same time as the temple destruction that the Roman Empire was at the peak of its grandeur and population during the late first and in the early second centuries AD?

5) Was there a seventy-year period of open Christian persecution during the church age of Philadelphia-Rapture as well?

6) Is it really such a coincidence that the church age of Philadelphia as mentioned in Revelation 3, had thus began with the death of the founding Latter-Day Saints' Mormon prophet, Joseph Smith, on June 27, 1844, and had ended exactly seventy years later with the death of Austrian Archduke Francis Ferdinand on June 28 in the year of 1914?

Diaspora Three

ITSO BELIEVES THAT THE DEATH of Ferdinand in 1914 had thereafter brought about the church age of Laodicea, our present age, and the beginning of World War I! Itso also believes that the three angels' messages of Revelation 14, while it does focus upon all seven of the churches in Revelation concurrently, do in fact refer to the last three end-time churches consecutively.

In other words, angel one warns the third last church of Sardis, or Protestant-Islam, of what will befall the entire world during the time of the church age of Philadelphia, or rapture. Great religious activity and persecution did occur during 1844 to 1914.

The second angel warns Philadelphia about what will befall the entire world during the church age of Laodicea, an age of which included two world wars. Finally, the third angel then arrives and warns the entire Laodicean world, or as Itso calls it, The Lukewarm Church of the Renaissance, of God's wrath to come upon them if he is continuously disobeyed by the time of the second coming of Jesus Christ!

Itso had continued to study the seven church letters in chapters 2 and 3 in the book of Revelation. Itso then had another question about church history: As there are three seventy-year diasporas which have occurred throughout earth's history, then how is it that only two of them are mentioned, and why?

For Itso to properly answer this perplexing question, he is to consider that the first Jewish diaspora of the Prophet Daniel's time had taken place centuries before the birth of Christ on earth. God the Father was the focus of judgment back then, instead of

God the Son, as would be the case in the following two diasporas centuries later.

Jesus Christ was, therefore, the revelator to John the Apostle of the seven letters to the seven churches. He had instructed John to write them in a book so that the letters could be sent out to each church.

By the time that Jesus was crucified, the first Jewish diaspora in Babylon had long since passed. Any mention of it at all, in Itso's opinion, would therefore have to be easily hidden in the first letter, which was indeed sent to the church of Ephesus!

What would the three historical seventy-year Jewish diasporas have in common with Itso or anyone else? Well, Itso had considered these three diasporas extremely important because they, throughout the ages and centuries, had indeed pointed directly to the three angels' messages, of which are found in Revelation 14!

Ezekiel the prophet, in the first chapter of his book by the same name of Ezekiel, mentions about wheels within wheels in the sixteenth verse of Ezekiel chapter 1, in the King James Version of the Bible. Itso had discovered that in the exact same way do the three angels' messages focus on the last and latest of the three diasporas, that being of Philadelphia, or rapture.

The Philadelphia-Rapture church-age diaspora of 1844 to 1914 is, in Itso's opinion, the one focal point of the three angels' messages of Revelation 14! It is also Itso's own belief that these messages do point directly to the second coming of Jesus Christ!

Another thing that Itso believes is that each of the three angels' messages of Revelation 14 are somehow related to and connect with that of the called, chosen, and faithful ones mentioned in Revelation 17:14. More revelation to come on this.

World Trade Center

Itso had remembered the first terrorist attack on the World Trade Center in New York City, February 1993. At that time, however, Itso had remained very skeptical about decoding Bible passages to make them look like modern-day newspaper headlines. Nevertheless, Itso had decided to take a deeper look at the "Got to go to sleep now" passage that Itso had received many years earlier from God.

Where there any hidden messages or meanings contained in this particular statement that Itso had previously overlooked? When Itso had fervently prayed to God for an answer, He had allowed Itso to concentrate only on the consonants of *g, t, t, g, t, sl, p, n,* and lastly, the consonant *w*.

Upon further deep meditation and prayer, Itso slowly began to see an entirely new message emerging. It was a message which read like this: "Great twin towers gone, terrorist slaughter people, New York City."

Great twin towers gone? Well, that made absolutely no sense to me at all! Itso thought. *Sure, there was a tragic terror attack of people in New York City, but hey, the twin towers were still standing!*

In May of 1998, Itso had attended a prophetic conference at a local high school in Barrie. This conference dealt with, among other things, the topic of hidden Bible codes. Itso's natural skepticism for coded messages and hidden meanings remained not only intact but increased Itso's assumption that if anything significant had not already happened yet concerning prophecy, then it would thus probably not happen.

On September 11, 2001, everyone knew what had happened. The two twin New York City towers had collapsed. It was only as Michael had predicted to Itso that they would, seventeen years earlier, back in May of 1984. Itso obviously was not meant to fully understand what Michael had already warned Itso about until many years later at this time.

Repeating Numbers

WHAT IS REALLY AMAZING ABOUT all of this? Well, when Itso had counted all of the consonants and vowels in Michael's quote of "Go to go to sleep now," Itso had found a total of seventeen letters. One letter for each consonant and vowel representing a one year's passage worth of time!

From what passage of time was Itso talking about? About from when Itso had last spoken to Michael face to face on the bus back in May of 1984. Itso had looked forward in time and right up to September 11 of 2001, for a total passage of seventeen years!

Itso had considered possibilities also as to why "Got to go to sleep now," was repeated again once. From the time of 1967, when Itso had his first visions of Michael, until 1984, when Itso saw once more of him, would thus constitute a passage of the first seventeen years. Year 1984 until 2001 would thus constitute the time span of another seventeen years. Both identical timespans added together total thirty-four years, or thirty-four letters, from 1967 until 2001!

When Itso had counted the sum of letters in "Got to go to sleep now," repeated once, Itso now had a total of thirty-four letters. Itso simply added together the two whole numbers of three plus four. The number of thirty-four is thus reduced to seven. Seven is therefore the universal number for God's perfect completeness!

Another way that Itso had put two whole numbers together was to reduce seventeen letters of "Got to go to sleep now," repeated once, to the equation of one plus seven equals eight. Eight multiplied by two is sixteen. One plus six, when both are added together, equals seven!

Itso could see, that seven vowels in Pitted Sunflower Seeds and in "Got to go to sleep now," repeated once, thus had indicated not only of God's total completeness, but also of the truth in his creation. Itso had earlier stated that the number seven is mentioned quite often in the Bible and is especially mentioned in the Bible books of Genesis, Daniel, as well as in the book of Revelation.

Itso had also noticed a total of twenty consonants in "Got to go to sleep now," repeated once. Of all the vowels in between the consonants, Itso had noticed that letter *e* is letter number five in the alphabet while *o* is the letter number fifteen. Five plus fifteen is twenty. The number twenty would later have turned out to be a significant time for Itso.

Emerging Patterns

By LATE APRIL OF 2001, Itso began to see certain patterns emerging in the vowels. Numbers such as seven and twenty were becoming especially evident.

With Michael's statement of "Got to go to sleep now," repeated once, Itso now had seven vowels each, for a total of fourteen vowels. Itso next added the seven vowels which are in Pitted Sunflower Seeds, for a total of twenty-one vowels. When Itso next added the four vowels in Saloon Nuts, Itso now had a total sum of twenty-five vowels. Two plus five in twenty-five now reduces that number to seven!

Itso could now see a pattern here. The handwriting was definitely on the wall, and Itso was more than merely talking about a cliché!

Itso had turned to the Bible book of Daniel 5:25–28. There, Itso had found the four words of handwriting as was witnessed by King Belshazzar and his court many centuries ago.

Itso had again used the one-letter-per-year principle as Itso had indicated earlier with the letters of "Got to go to sleep now." For all seventeen words with the sum of twenty-five vowels, Itso used this principle.

Which seventeen words do Itso refer? They are none other than the seventeen words put together, which refer to Saloon Nuts; Pitted Sunflower Seeds; Got to Go to Sleep Now, Got to Go to Sleep Now.

When the numbered sequencing of those twenty-five vowels is broken down, Itso, therefore, had number, number, weight, and division in reverse order! The three sevens are the universal numbers of completeness in heaven, while four is the earth number and its divisions!

Seven years on from 1984, and we have Gulf War I and the Soviet Union's collapse both in 1991. That year also, Itso completed the first of a few Bible prophecy correspondence courses that he would later complete in subsequent years.

Seven years from 1991, Itso attended the prophetic Bible-code conference in 1998. Nuclear watchdog inspectors from the United Nations had also withdrawn from Iraq in that same year. Seven years on from the Bible-code conference, and you have the death of Pope John Paul II in the year of 2005.

Itso then added four more years onto 2005 from the earth number of Saloon Nuts. This takes Itso to the year of 2009. When Itso added the twenty-five years worth of vowels onto 1984, Itso had thus reached the sum of 2009!

Will the year of 2009 indicate a major worldwide event to take place, and can this event point to the second-coming of Christ? With the passage of time, Itso would certainly know.

The Right Direction?

ITSO HAD WONDERED BY NOW why Michael would revel to him in reverse, or backward order, the number-number-weight-and-division sequence of Daniel chapter 5. The very order of Saloon Nuts; Pitted Sunflower Seeds; and Got to go to sleep now, got to go to sleep now does indeed indicate to Itso the backward order of division, weight, number, number. More specifically, what Itso does mean by the term "backward order," is the division of the saloon nuts, the weight of the pitted sunflower seeds, the number of "got to go to sleep now," and the number of "got to go to sleep now," as the word *number* itself was once repeated.

In Itso's opinion, there can be only one explanation for the phenomenon that he had indeed witnessed. Those who are in direct obedience to God are going in one direction, which is the right one, while those in direct disobedience to God are going in the exact opposite direction, that being, as you have guessed it by now, the wrong one!

Itso had illustrated further that whether or not one is going in the right direction toward God can be discovered by more research. The revised copyrighted 1980, eighth edition, seventh printing in 1984, of the booklet, *The United States and Britain in Prophecy*, had a very interesting chapter 4. It is entitled, "The Separation of the Birthright and the Sceptre."

In this chapter, Itso had found a clear distinction in meaning and in definition of birthright versus scepter. The spiritual promises of the scepter come from the Kingdom of Heaven while the material and national promises of the birthright come from the earth. In other words, the "grace" of the scepter versus the "race" of the birthright!

Itso did remember about the three seventy-year Jewish diasporas that he had earlier mentioned. Itso's understanding of number, number, weight, division can also be applied to all of these three diasporas and throughout history:

1) the number of Jews present in the Babylonian diaspora,
2) the number of Jews present in the Roman diaspora,
3) the weight of the Kingdom of Heaven present in the latter-day Philadelphia diaspora and tribulation,
4) the division of the birthright from the scepter at the second coming of Jesus Christ,

Division, weight, number, number had, in Itso's view, a different meaning and interpretation:

1) "Divisions" of birthright upon the earth, of which are many, include religious, secular, and national.
2) The "weight," as already mentioned, is of the holy Kingdom of Heaven upon the latter-day Philadelphia diaspora and tribulation.
3) The first "number" is of those present in the rapture of the true church into heaven.
4) The second "number" is of those present in the resurrection of the true church into heaven.

From Itso's point of view, all are united under the scepter of God, the scepter of grace. There are no divisions between Jews, Greeks, Christians, or Muslims under the scepter of God, as we would know these divisions within the birthright, or race. The scepter refers to immortal man, which are the heavenly angels. The birthright refers to mortal man, who are ruled over by fallen angels.

Why would Itso even mention about fallen angels at all? It is because their failed attempt to overthrow the kingdom of heaven had caused their legions to be permanently expelled from the presence of God, and to await God's further and also future judgement (Jude 6).

Itso could sense the influence of their rule upon this earth today. See Isaiah chapter 14, King James Version of the Bible.

History had already taught Itso about the defeat of the axis powers. Fine to say that Germany, Italy, and Japan, who together had formed the axis, were soundly defeated by the allied powers back in World War II.

Itso's chief concern and opinion today is that the cancerous growth of fascism, and that also does include the ugly stepsisters of racism and selfishness, have never been fully defeated by the allies of the Second World War. At best, the ugly cancer of fascism could only be temporarily kept in restraint, or in check. If there were no lingering fascist cancer, then there would have been no reason for the Cold War to exist between the communist East and the capitalist West as Itso had once known them to be.

We were supposed to be living in the post–Cold War age, were we not? thought Itso.

It is, therefore, Itso's opinion that the "serpent-cancer" of fascism had once again raised its ugly head. Only this time, on a much more subtle, cunning, and widespread manner than was ever before in our history. Itso then wondered about the end of this "mysterious wickedness," as the Bible calls it, which is currently infecting the entire world like the old, strange, and terrible disease that it is.

Another world war number three to suddenly erupt? thought Itso.

Itso did not confuse this war, the Nuclear War of Armageddon, with its final and climatic Battle of Armageddon, which is separated by three and a half years. This, the battle of Armageddon, is when, in Itso's opinion, all fascist forces unite to try and prevent none other than the second coming of Jesus Christ and the millennium!

Itso did find mentioned in the book, *1984* by George Orwell, that the worldwide caste or class system is divided into three general levels. The top level is the "inner party"; the middle level, the "outer party"; and at the bottom level, the "proletariat." These are better known in the Western world as the upper, middle, and lower classes. Too, the book *1984* is a story about how dark forces go about in their influence of the entire world.

It seems not like any coincidence to Itso that the latest publication dates of three books in Itso's possession does so happen to be in 1984. Those three books, whereby Itso makes reference to and had mentioned, are:

1) *The United States and Britain in Prophecy,*
2) *1984,* and
3) *New World Translation of the Holy Scriptures.*

In the Bible book of Genesis chapter 1, Itso had found where God had created the earth in six days. By the first three verses that begin chapter 2, Itso had found that God rested on the seventh day. From an evolutionary point of view, those six days can easily be watered down to make them sound like they are in fact, "six periods of time, each period of which is millions of years old"!

Itso does believe that when it comes right down to the seventh day, however, there really does seem to be a big problem with the evolutionary model of the passage of time. A day to God in scripture really is like the passage of a thousand years instead of countless millions of years. For example, any artifact, or object, which is unearthed from the soil may "appear" to be millions of years old, but that does not mean that they "are" millions of years old.

The epitome of all dark forces which do rule this earth today, Itso believes, would have to be those four horsemen of the apocalypse. These are detailed in the King James Version of Revelation chapter 6:2–8.

In a lead up to the section on the four horsemen, Itso's next focus is about the millennium itself. The millennium is the one thousand years of rest from God's six days of creation, which does compose God's seventh day of rest! This is in line with Revelation 20:2–3.

Three Millennium Concepts

"Okay, so we already know these are dark forces that role the earth throughout history and up to our present time." Thought Itso. "What about the worldwide millennium that each of these horses are pointing toward?"

Millennium concept one, is a "premillennial view" of the Messiah's return and the Messianic Kingdom in Hal Lindsey's book, "The Rapture: Truth or Consequences," that Itso had earlier mentioned. On page 27 of his book, Hal Lindsey mentions, there is general agreement in prophecy about a literal seven years of world tribulation. Also mentioned, is Jesus's return to establish a literal one-thousand-year earthly kingdom over which he will rule and a final judgment that does occur at the millennium end, where eternity is set to begin.

In millennium concept two, is the "postmillennial view," that Itso had read on page 29 of Hal Lindsey's book. Postmillennials believe the church will overcome the world and bring the millennial period of peace and perfect environment to earth by itself. This is a view which is based on a severe mishandling of the prophetic scriptures, along with the allegorical method of interpretation used throughout, instead of the literal method of interpretation.

Millennial concept three, is the "amillennial" concept that Itso had discovered in the same book on page 29. It means no millennium. No millennium means no certain time of tribulation and no millennial kingdom. Jesus comes at history's end, as all believers and non-believers are brought to judgment, and eternity then begins.

Concept three is only arrived at by an allegorical method of interpretation, meaning that words are assigned a meaning other than what was normally accepted and understood when they were originally written. When Amillennialists realize that true prophetic interpretation is literal, grammatical, and historical then they will know that this method of interpretation will indeed produce a pre-millennial view.

Itso believes that "amillennialism" is of the Antichrist doctrine while "post millennialism" would be therefore of false prophecy. The one true millennial doctrine, as is mentioned, and in Itso's opinion could only be therefore that of millennium concept one, is of a pre-millennial view!

"In such a larger historical context, where could I possibly be in terms of prophecy and the Second Advent of Christ?" Thought Itso. "May the four premillennial horsemen in Revelation 6:2–8 lead the way!"

Chapter 3

The Four Horsemen

Horseman One

Revelation 6:2, King James Version of the Bible, says, "And I saw, and behold a white horse: and he that sat on him had a bow; and a crown was given unto him: and he went forth conquering, and to conquer."

Now, to Itso, a crown in biblical prophecy seems to symbolize emperorship and kingship. Also, the bow is useless without an arrow to go with it. This points to the military weapon to choice commonly used in the time of Emperor Constantine the Great.

Itso had found that this weapon of choice required no arrows to be fired with this bow. It is none other than the weapon of compromise. When Itso had researched *The Encyclopedia Americana International Edition*, he found that it had this to say about Constantine the Great:

> "Constantine I (c.280–337 A.D.) Roman emperor, who is best known for his acceptance of Christianity and his transfer of the administrative center of the empire from Rome to Constantinople. He is usually referred to as 'Constantine the Great.'"

Constantine, Itso discovered, had joined his father Emperor Constantus at York in Britain, but by the summer of 306 AD, Constantus died; and the British legions hailed Constantine as Augustus. He had a bit of a struggle with other people to be named the supreme Augustus.

In 321 AD, Constantine thus invaded Italy and moved to Rome, encouraged by a vision of the cross against the sun. Rome was taken; he was supreme in the West and committed to his alliance with the Christians.

In the section entitled, "Constantine and Christianity," Itso found that *The Encyclopedia Americana International Edition* has this to say about Emperor Constantine the Great:

1) Constantine was not baptized a Christian until he lay upon his deathbed;
2) Undoubtedly considered himself in some manner a member of the Christian sect;
3) Played a major role in the church's affairs;
4) Afforded its members something more than toleration;
5) Non-technically, Constantine could be called the first Christian emperor;
6) Many of his family members were definitely Christians;
7) His mother Helene was extremely devout—she went on a pilgrimage to the Holy Land and promoted Church establishments both there and in Rome;
8) Constantine had credited his success to the divine message that he believed he had read in the skies just before the battle at the Milvan Bridge in the year of 312 AD;
9) Constantine could not, however, officially—and privately it seems he did not—abandon paganism at once;
10) Constantine did immerse himself into the church's affairs;
11) As Thirteenth Apostle, Constantine tried to unify the Christian community, divided as it was by doctrinal schisms;
12) Emperor Constantine defined orthodoxy not by merely refereeing these disputes, but by actually taking sides in them;
13) Embarked on his policy of toleration in 313 AD while also drawn into the battle over the Donatist schism in Africa;
14) Played a leading role in the 325 AD Nicaea Council occasioned by the Arian dispute, having divided the Christians in Egypt;

15) Possibly upon his counselor that of the Spanish bishop Hosius's opinion, Constantine did himself propose the formula of "homoousian," the consubstantiality of the Son and the Father, which was inserted in the Nicene Creed;

16) The Constantine-Christian alliance was of future importance for both partners, including that of the Roman government;

17) Both partners immediately benefited by the alliance when Constantine became emperor and the Christians were freed from persecution;

18) Union of church and state meant that political considerations would influence definitions of orthodoxy; and

19) The political decision of Constantine to abandon Rome for Constantinople was one of the reasons that lead to division between Eastern and Western churches.

In the paperback book entitled, *Nostradamus for Dummies*, Itso had read: "Early Christians faced persecution, but in 313 A.D., Christianity became the official religion of Rome under Emperor Constantine I when he signed the Edict of Milan."

Itso had found yet another source of information dealing with the legalization of Christianity in AD 313. In a special issue of *These Times*, "The amazing prophecies of Daniel and Revelation," it says on pages 24 and 25:

1) The experience of the entire church that followed 313 AD, when Christianity was legalized by Emperor Constantine, resembled that of the church at Pergamum.

2) Following this time, the church increasingly accepted pagan ideas and practices into its midst and advanced steadily down the path of apostasy foretold by Paul in 2 Thessalonians 2:3.

3) The Church's only hope lay in its willingness to let the sharp "two-edged sword" of truth wielded by Jesus cut away their selfishness and pride (Heb. 4:12).

Itso now had turned to the second chapter of Revelation to see why God hates the deeds of the Nicolations (verse 6) and the doctrine of the Nicolations (verse 15). *The World Book Encyclopedia*, Itso discovered, says that there were two Nicene councils—two councils of the Christian church held in Nices (now Iznik in northwest Turkey). The second Nicene Council was held in 787 AD for the purpose of settling a dispute governing the veneration of images:

1) Emperor Constantine, in 325 AD, had assembled the first council to settle the dispute caused by the Arian view of the Trinity.
2) Arius was an Alexandrian priest who believed that Christ is not of the same essence (personage) as God.
3) The council adopted the so-called Nicene Creed, which declared that God and Christ as God are of the same essence.
4) The council also fixed the time for observing Easter.
5) The Christian Easter in some places was held the same day as the Jewish Passover.
6) Other places had Easter observed on the following day of Sunday.

When Itso next had turned to *The Encyclopedia Americana International Edition*, Itso furthermore had discovered that it had these to say about the First Council of Nicaea:

1) It was the first ecumenical council in 325 AD held in Nicaea.
2) Constantine opened the council and participated in its deliberations.
3) The acts of the council were not preserved.
4) Only its creed, synodal letter, and twenty cannons survive.
5) the Nicene Creed had rejected the Arian's belief that the Son of God was separate from God the Father and that he was to be defined as the first of the Father's creatures.
6) The orthodox belief was strictly upon the consubstantiality (homoousic unscripturalness) of Father and Son, where the

sun, as God, is defined, but no clear distinction provided between Son and Father.

Itso had indicated already before of his belief that there is a clear distinction in personage between God the Son, Jesus Christ, and God the Father, the Archangel Michael. Itso had mentioned earlier about this clear distinction.

Itso had remembered how the prophet Daniel had interpreted to King Nebuchadnezzar about the great and terrible image that he saw in a dream. In the book of Daniel 2:45 in the King James version of the Bible, God says through Daniel, "For as much as thou sawest that the stone was cut out of the mountain without hands, and that it brakes in pieces the iron, the brass, the clay, the silver, and the gold; the great God hath made known to the King what shall come to pass hereafter: and the dream is certain, and the interpretation thereof sure."

Itso had considered in this verse the very possibility of how Jesus Christ, "the stone," was cut out or created from the mountain. The term "mountain" can easily be thus rendered to mean the "orb," or the "Kingdom of Heaven." "Without hands," therefore, would mean that Jesus Christ, the Savior of Itso, was created from the dust of the ground of the Kingdom of Heaven without human hands!

Itso had therefore believed that it was Jesus Christ who created the person of the Holy Spirit, or Adam, or the Archangel Michael from the dust of the ground of heaven before Christ had "planted" Michael in what the book of Genesis 2:8 describes as "a garden eastward in Eden." This "garden eastward in Eden" can also be rendered to mean, in Itso's own estimation, earth-universe in heaven, earth-paradise in heaven, or earth ruled by the sun in heaven!

Itso had now turned to Mark A. Findley's book, *The Almost Forgotten Day*. The last paragraph on page 57 states:

1) Sun worship gradually grew in prominence throughout the Roman Empire.
2) Though opposed at first, the Roman Emperor Aurelian, a third-century ruler from AD 270–275 had strongly supported sun worship.

3) It was the early fourth century when Christian Roman emperor Constantine had passed the first Sunday law on March 7, AD 321, that entitled Sunday as "the venerable day of the sun."

4) Church and state leaders had gradually unified in placing the emphasis from the true Bible Sabbath to its substitute day.

5) Early church leaders compromised when they gradually exalted Sunday in place of the true Bible Sabbath.

6) Nevertheless, Sabbath observance continued to be practiced.

7) Faithful warriors of God's truth were not willing to surrender the claims of God upon their conscience.

8) The Sabbath was more than merely days to these very champions as it was a matter of obedience to God.

When Itso then turned to a paragraph on page 60 of *The Almost Forgotten Day*, Itso had found that it said:

1) The attempted changeover of the Sabbath to Sunday had happened ever so slowly.

2) The first emergence of Sunday in Christian circles continued to be a day of work but included a worship service in honor of the resurrection.

3) It did not immediately take the place of the Sabbath for two hundred years (100–300 AD).

4) Sunday observance existed side by side with true Sabbath observance.

5) The trend set by Constantine and others, however, eventually did lead to the Sabbath change to Sunday.

So the change in God's worship from the Sabbath-day Saturday, the seventh day of the week, to Sunday, the first week-day, had become an ever so gradual process, thought Itso. *I have now wondered how all seven days on the weekly calendar had so come to be named. Who named them, and why?* was Itso's next question. It was not long before Itso had received the answers to this question.

In the book, *National Sunday Law* by A. Jan Marcussen, appendix 12, subtitled, "Time Not Lost," it says:

1) There have been many ancient calendars.
2) In 45 BC by Julius Caesar, was the first modern calendar as we have today put into use.
3) The names of days we have now were also used back then.
4) Babylonians worshipped the planets, so many had initiated the call of each weekday by the name of the planets.
5) The Hebrews and Bible writers never did this.
6) This was the reason that, although the day names we have today such as Sunday, Monday and so on had existed around the time of Christ, the Bible writers never referred to those days by these names because they were of pagan origin.
7) From Babylonian and Persian times, the old Mithra religion had led to the naming of the week days after the planets.
8) Zoroaster popularized in Persia around 630 BC, the god Mithra.
9) Roman soldiers had become worshippers of Mithra as it was supposedly a god of great courage.
10) Their travels allowed them to carry the idea to name each weekday after the planets among the Teutonic tribes better known today as Germany.
11) Even before the time of Christ, the Teutons had substituted a few of their own gods in place of planets for day names.
12) These names stuck, and they have been around ever since.
13) Here is a list, which names the Teutonic gods, along with the days of our week:
    Sun—Sunday
    Moon—Monday
    Tiu—Tuesday
    Wooden—Wednesday

Thor—Thursday
Frigg—Friday
Saturn—Saturday

14) The week of seven days has never been altered even though the calendar is constantly being updated to compensate for the 365 days, 5 hours, 48 minutes and 47.8 seconds in the year.
15) Historians who wrote around and even before the time of Christ have referred to "the day of the sun" and "the day of Saturn."

Itso can see why it is that God was so angry with the Nicolations whom he had mentioned about in the Bible book of Revelation chapter 2. The very deeds of the Nicolations, in the letter to the church of Ephesus, had to have been planned beforehand. For the very doctrine of the Nicolations had to have been constructed by the time that Itso had continued to read further verses up to, and with the inclusion of the letter written to the angel of the church in Pergamum! Itso does happen to believe that there had to have been both a passage and progression of time in order for deeds to have been thus turned into doctrine!

Itso's conclusion here is that where there are deeds, and then there will be creeds. Itso also believes that when it comes down to the trinity of God, as the Bible mentions, and then it would be really unwise to go against God's unchangeable ways of character. Itso therefore knows that God is no fool, so it would make absolutely no sense for Itso to be deemed a fool unless that it was by Itso's own disobedience directed toward God.

Although God is merciful by nature, Itso believes that God's mercies do not prevent him from allowing a curse on all who insist upon Sun worship and thereby usurp the very place of God's worship which is in heaven. Revelation 2:14 describes two high priests by the names of Balaam and Balac who each had committed the very mistake of sun worship.

Wasn't this what the second Nicene Council was about? thought Itso. *That "stumbling block, or curse," can therefore only lead to idolatry, fornication, and its close relative, adultery!*

Itso had now observed how Augustine's influence had brought about the rise of the Romanist church. Hal Lindsey had mentioned that Augustine's book, *The City of God*, taught:

1) Prophecy must be interpreted allegorically instead of literally;
2) Allegorical Prophecy had meant that the study of prophecy itself was cast into darkness for nearly a thousand and four-hundred years;
3) It was a book that influenced the Papacy for hundreds of years; and
4) The Papacy still holds most of Augustine's views.

The book, *National Sunday Law*, in chapter 3, subtitled, "The Beast Described," further describes both the rise and the fall of the Papacy. Itso read that:

1) "And the dragon gave him his power, and his seat, and great authority." (Rev. 13:2)
2) "Emperor Justinian 'gave' Rome to the Pope when he decreed that the Pope should be over all the Christian churches of the earth, and established the Papacy in 538 A.D., when the Emperor's general Belisarius drove the Ostrogoths from Rome."
3) "Rome gave him his 'seat.' Bible prophecy predicted it hundreds of years before it happened!"
4) "From 538 A.D., the Papacy ruled for exactly 1,260 years, until 1798 when something incredible happened. The Pope was taken prisoner! Napoleon's general, Berthier, captured the Pope and took him to France!"
5) "A deadly wound. The Papacy had reigned exactly 1,260 years. Could it have been a coincidence? Why did Berthier do it?

6) "Napoleon wanted to rule the world. The Papacy stood in his way. I wonder if they knew that they were fulfilling prophecy in spite of themselves!"

Itso had now moved on to the next premillennial horseman, that being the red horse. Itso was very interested in what this horseman had to say!

Horseman Two

IN THE BIBLE BOOK OF Revelation 6:4 of the King James Version, it says, "And there went out another horse that was red: and 'power' was given to him that sat thereon to take peace from the earth, and that they should kill one another: and there was given unto him a great sword."

Itso believes that the second horseman, and red horse of the apocalypse, in the book of Revelation is an apt description of Napoleon Bonaparte who became Emperor Napoleon I of France in 1799. This verse also covers all of the Napoleonic wars, which was his trademark.

Does this red-colored horseman sound a lot like Napoleon Bonaparte to Itso? Itso read what *Encyclopedia Americana* had to say about this man. Under the subheading entitled, "Peace and Reform," it says:

1) "He gave France needed peace by treaties with Austria and Britain, and a concordat with the Pope."
2) "He invited virtually all exiles to return—royalists and Jacobins—and formed a government of all talents."
3) "He began reforms that permanently affected French administration, finances, and education and gave life to the Louvre Museum and the Bibliotheque National."
4) "Napoleon presided over 57 of 102 meetings of the commission that produced the Code Napoleon, still the basic law of France."

Under the subheading of "Man and Legend," Itso had discovered that *Encyclopedia Americana* also says:

1) Napoleon was creditably both a dictator and a tyrant;
2) he was also perhaps the greatest enlightened monarch who had ever lived, and probably the greatest general;
3) he had an enormous impact on the history of Europe and the world, and his influence is felt even today.

When Itso turned to *The World Book Encyclopedia*, he found that it had this to say about Napoleon on page N-16:

1) Napoleon is both a historical figure and a legend—and it is sometimes difficult to separate the two.
2) Napoleon was one of the greatest military commanders in history.
3) He was also portrayed as a power-hungry conqueror.

Itso did see on pages N-17 and 18 what *The World Book Encyclopedia* says about the Napoleonic Wars:

1) Napoleonic wars (1796–1815) were a series of military campaigns led by Napoleon Bonaparte, a French general, who became Emperor Napoleon I of France.
2) From the late 1700s to the early 1800s, Napoleon conquered much of Europe and created an extensive empire.
3) Numerous factors, including his endless ambition and rising nationalism in the areas he conquered, had finally led to his downfall.

Itso did read beneath the subheading of "The Empire of Napoleon I," on page N-19 of *The World Book Encyclopedia*, which says:

1) Napoleon became the ruler of France in 1799.
2) By 1812, his empire covered most of Europe.

3) Napoleon was defeated at Leipzig in 1813 and was forced to give up the French throne in 1814.

4) He later formed another army but was defeated at Waterloo in 1815.

Another book read by Itso entitled, *Visions of Nostradamus and Other Prophets*, by author Donald Wigal, at the bottom of page 31, states that:

1) "Some say Nostradamus used an anagram for Napoleon in Century VIII, Quatrain I (Pay, Nay, Loron), while others claim the following (Century I, Quatrain 60) refers to Napoleon's reign: 'An emperor will be born near Italy who will cost the empire very dear. The people with whom he mixes will say he will be found less of a prince than a butcher.'"

2) "While Napoleon was thought to have brought France its first stable government in over a decade, the Napoleonic Wars were devastating to France, resulting in a great number of casualties."

Itso himself had discovered that there had to be something about Nostradamus's "Century I, Quatrain 60." When Itso had looked at a 1953 volume of *The New World Family Encyclopedia*, under the subtitle of "Napoleon I," he noticed that it had said: "Emperor of the French, born in Ajaccio, Corsica, Aug.15, 1769; died on the island of St. Helena, May 5, 1821. He was of a good Corsican family of Italian lineage."

On page 21 of Perry Kane's book, *Nostradamus and the Millennium: What May Be Coming*, there contains two of Nostradamus's quatrains. When Itso studied together these two quatrains, they would appear to him as the description of Napoleon Bonaparte to be the first of three antichrists that Nostradamus does describe for the end-times. The two quatrains put together one right after the other—Century 4.54 and then Century 4.82 both read like this:

1) "Holding a name which never belonged to a French King, there was never so fearful a thunderbolt Italy, Spain and the English tremble He will be greatly attractive to foreign women." (Century 4.54)

2) "A mass (of men) will draw near coming from Slavonia The Destroyer will ruin the old city He will see his Romania quite deserted Then will not know how to extinguish the great flame." (Century 4.82)

From the top of quatrain 4.54, Itso had easily interpreted Nostradamus's description of a name never before held by a French king as that of Napoleon Bonaparte. Perry Kane then goes on to say that Napoleon in Greek means "the new destroyer." Napoleon Bonaparte as first antichrist, Itso believes, is therefore tied to the first of the "three great woes," as they are found mentioned in the Bible book of revelation chapter 8, and in the last verse, verse 13. It now becomes quite plausible in Itso's view that these three biblical woes are a description of none other than the second, the third, and the fourth apocalyptic horses from Revelation 6:2–8!

The angel of the abyss in Revelation 9:11, Itso believes, is now tied to this first great woe. This "abyss angel" is then referred to by the name of "Apollyon," a word in ancient Greek meaning, "destroyer." Apollyon, in Itso's opinion, does sound much like that of Napoleon but without the *N*, of course! Another rendering of Apollyon thus would also sound quite similar to the term "abomination of desolation." Itso had discovered the term "abomination of desolation" in his reading of the eleventh verse in the book of Daniel chapter 12.

In the bottom, second quatrain of 4.82, Itso reads that Perry Kane then apparently talks about "The Destroyer" (Napoleon) ruining "the old city" of Moscow and sacking Rome to the point of it being deserted. He mentions about a possible nuclear problem to occur after the year two-thousand, so this covers the last line of Century 4.82.

With the possibility of nuclear war on the horizon, therefore, Itso was brought to the same conclusions. Was history doomed to repeat itself again? Will we have another magnetic, atomic war similar to the one which anciently erupted after the prophet Enoch and his church were taken up into the Kingdom of Heaven? (Gen. 5:22–24, Rev. 8:1–12)

Before Itso had moved on and away from Napoleon and to the third premillennial horseman, it did seem agreeable to Itso that the "great sword," which Napoleon carried with him, had been very impressive to watch indeed. The sword as a weapon of choice, and ever a symbol of warfare in the Bible, had reached its greatest extent of its effectiveness during the Napoleonic Wars.

It is anyone's guess, Itso's included, that the "three great woes" mentioned in the book of revelation is actually a description on the appearance of three premillennial antichrists in a specific sense. If anyone so happens to believe that the "three great woes" of Revelation 8:13 are directly and only linked to the appearance of the four horsemen of the apocalypse, then it is easy to render the first antichrist as Constantine; the second antichrist as Napoleon, and the third antichrist as Hitler. The fourth woe, or antichrist, would only be identified to the world upon the arrival of the great tribulation and the second coming of Jesus Christ!

There are those whom Itso believes, would not agree that Emperor Constantine the Great, though a white premillennial horseman, should be even considered an antichrist. If this is the case, and Itso considers some to be in this group, then it is easy to see why Napoleon would be considered the first antichrist of history, and not Constantine!

On page 19 and 20 of his book, *Nostradamus and the Millennium: What May Be Coming,* Perry Kane comments on another of Nostradamus's quatrains, that of Century 4.96:

> "The elder sister of the island of Britain will be
> born fifteen years before her brother because of
> his promise proving to be true. She will succeed
> to the Kingdom of the Balance."

Itso had now paid close attention to any mention of the balance! This is definitely a symbol which is featured prominently with

Premillennial Horseman Three, of Revelation 6:5 and 6! Here, following in point form, is Itso's interpretation of Perry Kane's commentary on Nostradamus's quatrain of Century 4.96, which in Itso's opinion is definitely a very good one:

1) The thirteen colonies of the 1700s, the so-called elder sister, struck out on their own officially in 1776.
2) France is America's brother.
3) France and England were enemies during the American Revolution.
4) France had excellent relations with the young Americans.
5) The French promised to help the Americans, and in 1781 with the Colonial Army Defeating Cornwallis' troops at Yorktown and unable to escape to the sea because the French fleet had them trapped, the British surrendered.
6) America thus became the first great modern democracy (the Balance), whose principle is a land governed by laws not men.
7) The balance—Libra—is America's judicial symbol.
8) Fifteen years after America's independence was when France, her younger brother, had its own constitution ratified in 1791.

It is now so plain to see where Itso is going with Nostradamus's Century 4.96. For another opinion on Nostradamus's 4.96, Itso does refer to the book entitled, *Nostradamus Prophecies for America*, by David Ovason in the chapter subtitled, "Britain, America and France," pages 63–69. There is reason for Itso to believe, therefore, that "the Kingdom of the Balance," America, is indeed a prominent symbol pointing to the third premillennial horseman!

Horseman Three

REVELATION 6:5 SAYS, "AND WHEN he had opened the third seal, I heard the third beast say, come and see. And I beheld, and lo a black horse; and he that sat on him had a pair of balances in his hand."

Itso has learned that from Napoleonic times through to our century, America as the Balance, represented the first great modern democracy with the principle of land governed by laws instead of men. Between World Wars I and II, this very principle was under a severe test due to the rising tide of authoritarian rule worldwide known to be the tide of fascism.

Balances to Itso, thus also represented a great need for world leaders to get the global trading system to function normally again as a result of the great depression of the 1930s. This was the same economic depression that had brought Germany's Adolf Hitler to power in the year of 1933.

Itso believes Revelation 6:6 is a more detailed description of who was affected by the great depression. Food shortages were common then, so food itself was weighed in soup kitchens very carefully. With Itso's emphasis in brackets, Revelation 6:6 says, "And I heard a voice [God] in the midst of the four beasts say, A measure of wheat for a penny, [a slice of bread] and three measures of barley for a penny: [barley soup, from soup kitchens] and see thou hurt not the oil and the wine [upper and middle classes]."

History reveals to Itso that it was the working class which was most affected by the food shortages. Coincidently also, it was the most swollen class by numbers due to massive unemployment. A rendering of soup kitchens doling out a slice of bread for a penny and three ladlesful of barley soup for a penny is quite evident though. The "oil" of the aristocracy and the wine of middle-class professions had remained largely unaffected by the great depression.

Here is why, therefore, Itso believes that the third premillennial horseman on the black horse of the apocalypse in revelation 6 does point directly to Adolf Hitler. In *The World Book Encyclopedia*, volume *H*, pages 264–265, it says:

1) Adolf Hitler was born in April 20, 1889, in Braunau, Austria, a small town across the Inn River from Germany.

2) In 1913, Hitler moved to Munich, Germany. The Austrian Army called him for a physical examination, but he was found unfit for service.

3) World War I began in August 1914. Hitler volunteered immediately for service in the German Army and was accepted.

4) But Hitler had risen only to a corporal's rank.

5) When Germany did surrender in November of 1918, Hitler was in a military hospital. He was recovering from temporary blindness, resulting from exposure to mustard gas when on the battlefield.

6) When Hitler received news of the armistice, he was deeply shaken.

7) Hitler was shocked by the armistice news because he believed that the cohesiveness of the German nation was under threat, and that he must attempt to save Germany.

8) Adolf Hitler (1889–1945) ruled Germany as dictator from the years of 1933–1945.

9) He turned Germany into a powerful war machine and provoked World War II in 1939.

10) Hitler's forces conquered most of Europe before they were defeated in 1945.

Incidentally, Itso had used an atlas to research the place of Braunau, Austria, where Hitler was born. Itso discovered that the Inn River is definitely a tributary to the Danube River and is not very far from the city of Munich, Germany. To some, the exact location of Hitler's birth does figure prominently, especially when it comes down to the seer Nostradamus's Century II, Quatrain 24 and its true and proper interpretation.

Itso had also discovered these about Hitler's rise to political prominence and dictator in *The World Book Encyclopedia* on page 267:

1) Paul von Hindenburg, the president of Germany, named Hitler "chancellor" (prime minister) on January 30 of 1933.
2) By the summer of 1933, Hitler had thus made himself dictator.

How did Adolf Hitler rise to dictator over Germany in such a short time after he had become its chancellor? Itso now had to ask himself.

In his quest to satisfactorily answer this question, Itso did look under the subtitle of "Dictatorship: 1933–1945," in volume 14, on page248 of *The Encyclopedia Americana International Edition*, which does have these to say:

1) The conservatives had deluded themselves into thinking that they could use Hitler for their own interests.
2) It was only within four months that Hitler had dramatically established his complete dominance over the conservatives and over all other political groups.
3) He had destroyed the communist and socialist parties and the labor unions.
4) He had forced the bourgeois and the right wing parties to dissolve.
5) He had emasculated or destroyed the paramilitary organizations.
6) He had eliminated the federal structure of the republic.
7) On March 23, 1933, Hitler had won from a decimated and intimidated Reichstag an enabling law that gave him dictatorial powers.

8) Hitler's success did come from a mixture of pseudo-democratic mass demonstration, terror by the SA (Storm Troopers or 'Sturmabteilung"), and the Nazicontrolled police that intensified post February's Reichstag fire.

9) Hitler has a deceptively conservative program whose purpose was to keep the conservatives on the same page as Hitler.

As Itso continued to read on, Itso had discovered that Adolf Hitler was not satisfied with just merely being the dictator of Germany, though. Under the subtitle, "Consolidation of Power," volume 14, page 248, *Encyclopedia Americana* continues:

1) Hitler, in early 1934, had faced new conflicts mainly from within the Nazi party.

2) The Roehm led SA and the Nazi left vigorously were against Hitler's alliance with business and military leaders, even as monarchists, were working to restore the monarchy.

3) Hindenburg's worsening health thus posed the question of his succession.

4) Hitler had radically survived the crises as he rallied behind himself, the party leaders, the army, and Hitler's SS (the 'Schutzstaffel," or Blackshirts).

5) On June 30, 1934, Hitler had emerged as the undisputed master of Germany as a number of SA leaders, monarchists, and other opponents were murdered while the influence of the SA was drastically reduced.

6) On August 2, 1934, Hitler officially assumed the title "Fuhrer," or supreme head of Germany, upon Hindenburg's death on the same day.

7) Hitler had thus consolidated his dictatorship during the 1935–38 period.

8) The basis of Hitler's power continued to be his control over the masses who admired him as the "man of the people" and who had falsely credited Germany's economic recovery to him. (Hjalmer Schact, a conservative banker, was its real architect.)

9) So it was that in 1937–1938 that the economy of Germany had reached its full employment due to an increasingly reckless rearmament policy.

10) By promoting rivalries among his subordinates, Hitler had also protected his own position as the Fuhrer.

11) Hitler had encouraged Himmler to build a formidable apparatus of terror by means of the SS, the Gestapo, and the concentration camps.

12) He then escalated the persecution of the Jews through the Nuremburg Laws of 1935, which deprived Jews of their citizenship and forbade marriages between Jews and non-Jews.

As Itso had now learned about the events which had allowed Adolf Hitler to become the absolute dictator of Germany, Itso needed not to have gone into any great particulars about the horrible mess which had followed. (Ezekiel 23:23–26 has details.)

By April, 1945 the Russians were rapidly approaching Hitler's bunker in Berlin; and on April 30, 1945, Hitler had committed suicide.

Some believe that Adolf Hitler did not commit suicide in 1945 and faked his death. Whether plausible or not, the fact remains to Itso, that the Nazis went into hiding after World War II, only to emerge again at the right time.

Who could have foreseen the rise of this dictatorial tyrant before it was too late? Itso thought.

A possible answer to this question, in Itso's opinion, would have to be the sixteenth-century French prophet and seer, Nostradamus. Itso had mentioned already about Nostradamus's quatrains in connection to a previous tyrant who also had risen and fallen many years before Adolf Hitler did that is none other than Napoleon Bonaparte!

Itso turned next to *The World Book Encyclopedia*, volume *N*, on page 550. It had this to say about Nostradamus and the Nazis: "Nostradamus's prophecies are vague and open to interpretation. One prophecy seemed to predict World War II (1939–1945). During the war, the Nazis issued their own versions of Nostradamus's prophecies to convince the German people and their European enemies of the Nazis' ultimate victory."

Much the "Nostradamus and the Nazis" quote says to Itso. How easy it really is, not only for individuals to misinterpret the prophecies of Nostradamus but for entire governments to do the exact same thing. To Itso, therefore, it really does seem to matter that individuals are on the right or wrong side of the truth and that governments are on the right or wrong side of what history had to say!

Even in our modern twenty-first century, it still does seem to Itso that no two separate interpretations of Nostradamus's quatrains appear to entirely agree. Here are some examples of what Itso is talking about. One such example is illustrated nicely in Richard Smolley's book, *The Essential Nostradamus*. When Itso had read one of Nostradamus quatrains, Century II, Quatrain 24, it said this:

> "Maddened beasts to cross streams for hunger;
> Most of the camp will be against Hister,
> In a cage of iron the great one will have him
>   dragged,
> When the German child espies the Rhine."

Itso then went on to read Richard Smolley's commentaries about Century II, Quatrain 24, on page 85, which says:

1) "'Hister' is an antique name for the Danube River flowing through Austria, but many commentators have seized upon this as a premonition of Adolf Hitler, not only because of the similarity in names but on the grounds that Hitler was born in a town on the Danube."
2) "Unlike many attempts to fit Nostradamus into the Procrustean bed of recent events, this one actually bears some resemblance to historical fact."
3) "Indeed the greater part of the world eventually combined to fight Hitler, and the third line is sometimes taken to

refer to his ally, the Italian dictator Benito Mussolini, who did end up in a cage after his fall from power."

4) "The last line would then allude to Hitler's march into the Rhineland in 1936, which set the stage for World War II."

5) "Another reading of this line goes, 'Quand rien enfant Germain observera'—'When the German child sees nothing— which would point to the obliviousness of the German people to Hitler's evil motives.

6) "Nevertheless, the fit is not exact. Hitler was not born on the Danube. He was born in Braunau am Inn ("Braunau on the Inn"), which, as its name suggests, is on the River Inn, which is only a tributary of the Danube."

As was mentioned before, Itso had used an atlas to research the place of Braunau, Austria, where Hitler was born. Itso had discovered for himself that the Inn River is most definitely a tributary to the Danube River.

Another interpretation that Itso found of Century II, Quatrain 24, can be found in Donald Wigal's book, *Visions of Nostradamus and Other Prophets*. On the very bottom of page 31 and top-half of page 32, it says:

1) "Nostradamus's specific mention of the name Hister, which many take to mean Hitler, had sparked the interest of even the most skeptical over the last fifty years."

2) "Scholars of Nostradamus point to his frequent use of anagrams to refer to people and places, noting that he often replaced a single letter."

3) "Skeptics note that the word 'hister' was used by the Romans to refer to 'river.'"

4) However, river doesn't make a great deal of sense inserted into the quatrains in question.

5) "Here are two (quatrains) that were so remarkably like actual events that even the Nazis became paranoid:
   a) 'Century II, Quatrain 24 [Itso's emphasis is in brackets]—Beasts wild with hunger will cross rivers [Hitler's

invasion of France?]. The greater part of the field will be against Hister [Allies versus Axis?]. The great one will be dragged in an iron cage [Mussolini?]. When the child of Germany observes nothing [War tide against Hitler in Berlin bunker?].

b) 'Century V, Quatrain 94 [Itso's emphasis is in brackets]—He will transfer into greater Germany [Hitler's invasion of Belgium and France?] Brabant and Flanders, Ghent, Bruge, and Boulogne. The truce [sitzkrieg?], a sham, the great duke of Armenia [Winston Churchill?] Will attack Vienna and Cologne.'"

There was absolutely no doubt, therefore, in Itso's mind, when Itso had looked closely at these two quatrains, "Century II, Quatrain 24" and "Century V, Quatrain 94," why the Nazis would indeed become paranoid. When Itso had looked at an atlas, he discovered that the regions of Brabant and Flanders, as well as the cities of Gent and Bruge, are all located in Belgium. The city of Boulogne in France has a main road connecting to the capital city of Paris in the south. As with Napoleon and his army, Itso also had to wonder whether Hitler and his Nazis had known that they too were fulfilling prophecy in spite of themselves!

Overconfidence can certainly be quite a dangerous game when you are on the wrong side of history. Especially dangerous, as Itso had observed, would be any alteration and any slant of Nostradamus's messages for propaganda purposes!

To think that they, the Nazis, could be so confident of victory during World War II that they would choose to ignore the obvious! thought Itso.

There is yet, Itso had found, another possibility as to the true meaning of the term, "Hister." In the broadest sense, "Hister" can easily be rendered to mean "Historicist Premillennialism." Of the three historical millennial concepts that Itso had mentioned before, it is Itso's belief that millennium concept one, that of a premillennial view, is one which agrees with historicist premillennialism.

When Itso had revisited again the second line of Nostradamus's "Century II, Quatrain 24," it was then that Itso could begin to see that the term of "Hister" can indeed take on an entirely new and different meaning, which is beyond that of Adolf Hitler. In fact, the very line that does says, "The greater part of the field will be against Hister," is what Itso believes can also be rendered to mean, "The greater part of the earth will be against historicist premillennialism!"

History had proven to Itso quite well that the Nazis, with their public displays of Bible book burning, were not premillennialists in their thinking but amillennialists, as was explained earlier in more detail. Amillennialism, therefore, had been quite a dark horse indeed!

Not only does Itso believe the demonic doctrine of Amillennialism to be that of the Antichrist, Itso also believes that the demonic doctrine of postmillennialism is also that of false prophecy. In other words, "death" and "hell" that follows with it (Rev. 6:8)!

Of the four premillennial horsemen, which are of Revelation chapter 6 in the Bible, Itso believes that premillennial horseman four is the most mysterious of them all. Itso also believes that the true identity of this fourth horseman will not be revealed to the world until the beginning of the great tribulation which does precede the second coming of Jesus Christ!

Horseman Four

WHAT CAN ITSO MAKE OF the fourth horseman when Itso does not know yet of its true identity? There are some clues of which Itso could point to the fourth horseman's identity nevertheless! The King James Version of the Bible, Revelation 6:8 had this to say about the fourth horseman: "And I looked, and behold a pale horse: and his name that sat on him was death, and Hell followed with him. And power was given unto them over the fourth part of the earth, to kill with sword, and with hunger, and with death, and with the beasts of the earth."

As can be well imagined again, Itso had indeed many questions to ask about in regards to the true identity of, and the circumstances that surround, the fourth horseman of the apocalypse. It is Itso's hope that someday soon, Itso's questions will be satisfactorily answered, such as:

1) Does all of this sound to you like an eruption of another world war, World War III?
2) Power given to whom over the fourth part of the earth?
3) Could this mean that the forces of fascism are all that remain upon the earth after the rapture and resurrection of the church into the Kingdom of Heaven?
4) What about "the fourth part of the earth"?
5) Could this refer to the fact that three-fourth of a plant consists of its root systems growing beneath the surface of the earth while the "fourth part" is the trees and grasses that have to be seen growing above the surface?

6) A nuclear war to erupt upon the surface of the earth quite suddenly, therefore?

7) Does the term, "to kill with sword, and with hunger, and with death, and with the beasts of the earth," means, in fact, war, famine, disease, and military weapons of war?

What all of these seven questions do reveal to Itso is that, and very tragically, that man's inhumanity to man will most certainly appear to be at its very worst! The good news is that the remainder of the true church that remains upon the earth post-rapture will be given, despite widespread persecution, the tools necessary to survive the dark period and into the millennium (Rev. 6:9–11,11:7–10,14:13).

Some further questions now did suddenly come into Itso's mind. These questions, and Itso's attempt to answer them, have indeed something to do with the certain identity of the fourth horseman.

1) What are some clues which might point toward the possible identity of this fourth horseman?

2) Is the political entity of Magog, mentioned in The Old Testament book of Ezekiel 38:2 and 39:6 the same political entity as the prophet Nostradamus's mention of Mabus?

In a book entitled, *The Complete Prophecies of Nostradamus*, the name "Mabus," Itso found, is mentioned in one of Nostradamus's quatrains. "Century II, quatrain 62, on page 63, has this to say about Mabus:

"Mabus shall come, and soon after shall die,
Of people and beasts shall be a horrible destruction,
Then on a sudden the vengeance shall be seen,
Blood, hand, thirst, famine, when the comet shall run."

A commentary about this quatrain, with Itso's emphasis in brackets, has this to say: "The coming of the comet [scepter, orb of

Heaven?] shall occur in the period of reconstruction [Temple?] and there will be vengeance for the wrongs inflicted on humanity by self-ish interests [Testing time?]."

Itso himself had now focused upon Nostradamus's Century II, quatrain 62. About this quatrain, Itso had some questions to ask:

1) Is Mabus and Magog, therefore, the name of premillennial horseman four, the rider of the fourth horse of the biblical apocalypse?

2) Line two of the quatrain, says, "of people and beasts." Is this just another way for Nostradamus to describe civilians and military?

3) What exactly is "the vengeance" revealed in line 3 of quatrain 62 in Century II?

4) Does quatrain 62 therefore describe the great tribulation period before the second coming of Jesus Christ upon the earth?

5) Is Jesus Christ the vengeance coming upon earth to bring the sword of judgement upon the wicked (Ps. 94)?

6) Is the last line of quatrain 62 in Century II that says, "when the comet shall run," also a description of the great tribulation and the second coming of Jesus Christ?

Are there others of Nostradamus's quatrains which appear to talk about the second coming and a possible nuclear war? Itso believes that there are more quatrains. The *Complete Prophecies of Nostradamus*, Century VI, quatrain 24, on page 187, with Itso's emphasis in brackets, says: "Mars [War] and the sceptre [Heaven], being conjoined together, Under Cancer [July, Mabus?] shall be a calamitous war, a little while after a new king shall be anointed [second-coming?], who for a long time, shall pacify the earth [Millennial Kingdom?]"

The running commentary next to Century VI, quatrain 24, with Itso's emphasis in brackets, says this:

"Nostradamus here speaks of a constellation called the Sceptre. Looking far into the future [now approaching?], he foretells of a time when this constellation shall be in conjunction with Mars, and a terrible war that will break out under this influence. And out of this debacle there will arise a new world leader [Christ?] and peace will reign for a long time afterward [Millennium?]."

Another quatrain Itso had found was "Century IX, quartain 44" of *Complete Prophecies*. It is yet another quatrain which seems to give mention about the second coming of Christ and nuclear war. On page 292, and with Itso's emphasis in brackets, it says:

"Leave, leave, go forth out of Geneva, all Saturn of gold, shall be changed into iron, The Contrary of the positive ray [nuclear war?] shall extermi-nate all, Before it happens, the Heavens [second coming?] shall show signs."

In a commentary about Century IX, quatrain 44, Itso had dis-covered it does thankfully reveal that not all is to be gloom and doom: "Startling! Nostradamus here foretells the advent of atomic power. He indicates clearly that this force can be used for useful or destruc-tive purposes. But, with terrifying finality, he warns of the eventual destruction of our civilization by means of the release of atomic energy- holding out but one ray of hope, the Heavens shall show signs, meaning that we will be given one final chance to determine our destiny."

On page 34 in Donald Wigal's book, *Visions of Nostradamus and Other Prophets*, is Nostradamus's "Century X, quatrain 72." With the addition of Itso's emphasis in brackets, it says:

"The year 1999, seven months,
From the sky will come
a great King of Terror: [Horseman Four, False
    Prophet?]
To bring back to life

the great King of the Mongols, [Horseman Four,
    Antichrist?]
Before and after [the lesser tribulation?]
Mars [god of war] to reign by good luck [Syria?]."

There can be of no doubt in Itso's view that out in this world today, in all probability, exist several candidates who could fit the exact identity of the fourth apocalyptic horseman. The Feast of Unleavened Bread ends, while the Feast of Pentecost begins as the world takes no notice of this important event. With the European "Brexit" in June of 2016, followed by the election of a new U.S. President in November of 2016, Itso can now foresee a major world-wide economical shift beginning in December of 2016!

Itso now believes that the burial of Cuban leader Fidel Castro on December 4, 2016, following his death in November, has now brought the "Feast of Unleavened Bread'" to its entire stop as well as its ending. Castro's burial, now marks the opening phase of Daniel's first witness, as is mentioned about in the twelfth chapter of Daniel in the scriptures of the Bible. The first witness period, Itso believes, is therefore to last for exactly 1,290 days—until June of the year 2020.

It is a general question that still does remain, however, as to whether or not Germany will fall into the hands of the "Daesh" or the "Islamic State," sometime in 2017. The refuge crisis, in which Germany is currently experiencing, will be of absolutely no help to either Germany, Europe, or the rest of the world in the long run.

Itso does have more to say about the three-and-a-half-year reign of the beast power in the following fourth chapter. It is this beast power that is in itself symbolized by Itso's "iron statue" vision!

Chapter 4

The Statues of Great Tribulation

September Eleven

I<small>TSO DID REMEMBER WHAT HE</small> was doing on that fateful day of September 11, 2001. Most people will still remember where they were on that day when they first had heard the terrible news. Itso had turned on the radio and tuned into a radio station that morning as it reported that a small plane had crashed into Tower 1, of the World Trade Center in Manhattan.

Prompted thereafter to tune into a live broadcast of a New York City talk show that morning on television, Itso could now see much smoke billowing out from Tower 1. Thinking that it must have been an unfortunate accident, or an electric fire, Itso continued to watch for a minute or two until he witnessed what was another plane in the sky above.

The second plane did appear to hover almost motionless beside the second identical tower. From Itso's television vantage point, the jet plane could be seen directly at front, with its cockpit between its two circular jet engines.

How very odd that they should allow such a large aircraft to land on top of skyscrapers, Itso thought.

That was the point for which it had almost instantly dawned upon Itso. There were no such allowances for any type of plane to land on the top of the twin towers!

An English translation from Nostradamus's Century VI, quatrain 97 could not be described any better, unless Itso was actually witnessing these horrific events directly from the television screen as they were actually taking place. In his book, *Nostradamus—Prophecies for America*, David Ovason has this very verse from Century VI, listed under the subheading, "The Attack on Manhattan," page 14, with Itso's emphasis in brackets:

> "Five and forty degrees the sky will burn [Smoke
>   from Tower 1?],
> Fire to approach the great new city [jet aircraft?],
> Within an instant, a great flame will leap like light-
>   ning [Tower 2?],
> When one would wish the Normans to give trial
>   [America, the balance?]."

On September 11, 2001, Itso thus began to revisit the ten consonants of "Got to go to sleep now," to see whether or not a new blog or newspaper headline would now begin to emerge. A new headline had emerged that day, which was only slightly different from the earlier one that was dated back to February 1993:

> "Great Twin Towers Gone;
> Terrorist Slaughter, People;
> New York City, Washington D.C."

Only with the passage of time since September 11, 2001, did Itso begin to discern a new and far more ominous message:

> "Giant Tidal Tsunami Generated;
> Terrible Slaughter, English Earthquake;
> Pentagon, Nuclear War."

Well, that made absolutely no sense to me at all! Itso thought. *Sure, there was a tragic terror attack on the Pentagon, but hey, the Pentagon is still standing. What small damage to the building that there was, has been long since repaired!*

Previously having mentioned that the Christian word for *sleep* had meant *death*, Itso began to focus on the word *sleep* as it is in "Got to go to sleep now." Between *sl* and *p*, there are two *e*'s. These two *e* vowels represent the fifth letter of the alphabet, just as the

Pentagon itself is a five-sided building. Itso did next render those two *e*'s together to form one single ten-letter word. That single, ten-letter word spells *earthquake*.

Does this mean that at some future time, there is to be another terrorist attack on the Pentagon by an earthquake? If so, when? Itso had wondered.

As Itso was merely a mortal human being here on the earth like everyone else, Itso knew that he was no angel. Itso knew that he was bound and tied to the laws of time and unforeseen circumstances as was all mortals in this world.

What did God mean to tell Itso here? Did God mean to say that not only were there two separate terrorist attacks which had completely destroyed the World Trade Centre Towers in New York City, but that there would be yet another terrorist type of an attack to destroy the Pentagon? Only with the passage of time itself will Itso know for certain.

Was God Himself, therefore, to blame for the fact that 9/11 had even happened? Itso's own personal answer to this question was an unequivocal no!

It was and continued to be Itso's true belief that God had allowed the disaster of 9/11 to occur. Also true was Itso's belief that God had warned Itso of 9/11 seventeen years prior to the horrific events.

Even if Itso did have the capacity to properly understand in time every sign given before the happening of 9/11 (or in Itso's case, all of the vowels and all of the consonants), would anyone have believed then that such a horror of 9/11 could ever happen? That there were obviously some very dark forces in play that day, is well known. So to say that God is to blame for the tragic events of nine-eleven, is in Itso's opinion, just plain wrong!

Itso was rest assured, that it is God Himself, who ultimately does determine the final outcome of every event such as nine-eleven. Itso had known that the providence of God never fails. Itso had also known that through him, God was the one who had sounded a general warning on what is to come.

Earthquakes, Radiation, and Disease

THE TERRIBLE EARTHQUAKE, TSUNAMI, AND nuclear crisis in Japan as of March 11, 2011, appears at first glance to be a unique situation of which our world has never experienced before. The uniqueness of the nuclear situation in Japan, however, should not be, in Itso's opinion, an event that is entirely new. Far from it.

Now Itso is of course not merely referring to the two atom bombs which were dropped on Hiroshima and Nagasaki. They had marked the end of World War II as well as the beginning of the atomic age in our world.

Most by now have seen films of radiation sickness which had resulted from the explosive aftermath of those atom bombs. Radiation sickness, that one can plainly see, involves blotchy skin, and profuse bleeding around the eyes, ears, nose, and also the mouth.

From a historical perspective, Itso believes that earthquakes, radiation, and disease go much further back into time than just merely the Second World War. The earth's core is what Itso had found as like a giant nuclear reactor which radiates its nuclear energy into the earth's crust at a constantly fluctuating rate. The Bible itself makes this fact absolutely plain to see when one reads about the sudden destruction of Sodom and Gomorrah found in the book of Genesis in the nineteenth chapter.

Jackdaw Fifty, on *The Black Death* sheet by E. R. Chamberlain, have much to say about the plagues of history, especially that of the Black Death in middle-age Europe. Itso has found that there are other examples of plagues in history which leave their own legacy behind.

In the third century BC, the Romans did record the presence of the plague in Africa. Plague also appeared in Constantinople in 542 AD, which had passed over all Europe in the next fifty years.

The sixth-century plague would also apply to a number of outbreaks happening over the next seven-hundred years, along with the fourteenth-century Black Death. This, in Itso's opinion, does correspond exactly with sudden spikes in radioactivity levels coming from the earth which could only be possibly produced by increasingly severe earthquakes and volcanic activity in the earth.

Major spikes in radioactivity levels coming from below earth would also be, in Itso's opinion, the direct cause of all plague outbreaks in every century up to and including our present day. Itso also believes that radiation spikes can turn what would normally be harmless viruses and bacteria into disease-producing killing machines. This would therefore apply equally to those microbes in both air and water

Could it be, therefore, that a major volcanic eruption and earthquake in far off China in the fourteenth century be the source of radioactivity, polluting the atmosphere, and thus turning normally harmless viruses and bacteria into monsters? Itso wondered.

There were caravans which had travelled many years along the notable trade routes between China and Europe. It is thus clear to Itso how radioactive fallout from the earth could have easily contaminated thousands of people and therefore would have spread the plague into Europe! Itso had noted that on the "II Diagnosis" sheet of Jackdaw number fifty, is a paragraph that states:

> "It was also believed that the series of violent earthquakes that disturbed southern Europe in the mid-fourteenth century contributed to the plague. The foul vapours engendered by Jupiter were supposed to have built up inside the Earth and eventually forced their way out, creating earthquakes and adding their quota of poison to the atmosphere."

This direct quotation speaks volumes about the effects of natural radiation vaporizing from the earth and its devastating effects on the entire food chain. Itso believes that any normal virus or bacteria in our environment that could suddenly turn deadly would thus depend upon the level of radiation present in our air and water!

With the exceptions of astronomers such as Copernicus and Galileo, there was not much of a concept in middle-age Europe that the planet earth itself could even be round in shape, as was other planets like Jupiter. Therefore, any mysterious mists or miasma suddenly appearing upon the earth would easily have the view of divine punishments from above, not below.

In modern-day terms though, Itso can now determine that while the plague punishments are divinely from above, the effects of these punishments had come from below. Punishments that are in the form of natural radiation and of which does pulsate directly from the earth's nuclear core.

Itso can now clearly see the connections of radiation to major earthquakes and other notable events. Examples of such events, among others, do include the London Plague of the year 1665, followed by the London Fire in 1666, and the Irish Potato Blight of the year 1845 to eighteen 1849.

Itso could also see that no two spikes in natural radiation levels all through history have therefore been identical in shape. Neither has the political or economic events these radiation spikes have influenced, nor any of the diseases they may have produced.

Itso had noticed, however, the continued modern-day examples between radioactive events and the appearance of new types of diseases. Is there any connection between "mad cow disease" that appeared in November of 1986 and the Chernobyl nuclear explosion in April the same year?

Nuclear energy itself, Itso believes, is exactly how God our Creator had control over not only planet earth but as well as our solar system, our Milky Way galaxy and every galaxy that is in the entire universe. It does not take much a leap of imagination for Itso to realize also that on the cellular atomic level, the behavior of cells can and do resemble those of planets and galaxies.

Black holes are also a reality, which does exist on both planetary and atomic levels. Itso believes that black holes are the boundary markers which give the universe with its cells and planets, their limitations.

The reason that Itso believes that this is so is that black holes, by their very nature, have the power to both create and to as well destroy at a constant rate both the cellular and the planetary levels. Black holes, by their very definition, are therefore both the entry and the exit points into and out of the Kingdom of Heaven!

Radiation from the earth's core, Itso believes, is therefore the process which switches on and off both the evolution and the disease-making microbes. Radiation spikes in world environmental history have been and continue to be due to earthquakes as well as volcanic activity.

Itso's Christ Vision

ABOUT SIX MONTHS BEFORE THE death of Itso's own parental father in late November of 2011, there was the vision of Jesus Christ. He was as the Apostle John had described him in the book of Revelation 1:14. His eyes really were as a flame of fire from a mortal point of having witnessed such a divine vision as this!

Itso was on his way to do some grocery shopping at the local plaza as he regularly does quite often. Walking ahead of Itso did he seem to be making what Itso describes as some strange-sounding, groaning noise. That was what first attracted Itso's attention, although Itso had pretended not to notice anything unusual.

Late afternoon in the early part of May, on a Thursday, it had been a typical spring day. Itso had continued to observe this rather stout male figure who was walking a short distance in front of Itso. Itso then had noticed that he wore a jacket, red in color, and dark-colored trousers. This male figure had continued to walk along the same side of the street and was always ahead of Itso, as he had continued to maintain a short distance by a length of several feet.

It was then that Itso had noticed something rather odd was happening. He had suddenly held out to Itso in plain view, a large bottle of sarsaparilla coke. The bottle was upside down with the bottle cap still attached to hold all of the liquid in place.

Itso had to wonder now whether or not this had symbolized all of the issues of life that were kept in check by a single bottle cap. About future prophecy awaiting fulfillment? The pop bottle had now vanished.

Another odd thing Itso noticed was that the man had suddenly reversed his direction upon the sidewalk and was now walking in the opposite direction. He now was walking and coming directly toward Itso.

As he passed Itso, he nor Itso had said even a word to each other. Itso could easily see that his eyes burned like fire. Itso could not also simultaneously see the outline of his face for it was literally glowing at a level of intensity that appeared to be brighter than the sun!

He had looked like he was still there after he had gone past Itso, when Itso had looked behind him. Itso noticed that He had not suddenly disappeared from view but only gradually, as he walked farther away down the street. Itso had felt that there was not any physical collision between them at all, whatsoever, when he had passed by Itso.

Itso had continued to walk ahead and do the grocery shopping as if nothing unusual had happened along the way. Itso now had felt, however, that someone had obviously been in a watch over what he was doing on that day.

There remains one question for which Itso does continue to ponder about since that day. It is all about those plainly labeled letters on the soda bottle. The question is this: are the four letters, plainly labelled "Coke" on that soda bottle, an acronym that happens to stand for and is meant to read, "Christ Over Kingdom Eternal"?

Sabbath Day Remembrance

HAVING COMPLETED THE HERBERT W. Armstrong College Bible Correspondence course in the summer of 2013, there was a topic which became of particular interest to Itso. The subject is all about "Sabbath Day Remembrance."

In the King James Version of the Pentateuch, there are of two places where the Sabbath Day commandment is mentioned. The first is in Exodus 20:8. The second place is in Deuteronomy 5:12.

Exodus 20:8 says, "Remember the Sabbath day, to keep it holy." This remembrance of the Sabbath day goes together with the same fourth commandment mentioned in Deuteronomy 5:12, which says, "Keep the Sabbath day to sanctify it, as the Lord thy God hath commanded thee."

Itso had learned that it is this fourth commandment from God, more than any other, which points directly to the seven-day Sabbath cycle. Itso had also learned that he could juxtapose all the seven annual festivals of God's master plan for humanity's salvation. As a substitute for the pagan seven-day, Sunday-to-Saturday cycle, he could now actually "remember the Sabbath day, to keep it holy" of Exodus 20:8!

Meaning of Seven Annual Festivals

WHAT EXACTLY ARE THE "SEVEN Annual Festivals," and what do they mean? How connected are these seven festivals to the Philadelphia Church of God? This is what Itso would next be able to discover.

The first festival is that of Passover. It is a memorial of the sacrifice of Jesus Christ, "our Passover," which made possible the forgiveness of our sins. There are no holy days to this feast in particular.

The second festival is called the Days of Unleavened Bread. This festival portrays putting sin out of our lives and striving to obey God's commandments. This festival also portrays the church age, which precedes that of the one-thousand-year millennial age. There are two "holy days" to this feast, one on the "first" day and one on the "last day" of the festival.

The third festival is that of Pentecost. It depicts the church as the "first fruits" of salvation, the first to be spiritually begotten and born into God's family. This is a holy day. Itso likes to refer to this group as those who have been "raptured" into the Kingdom of Heaven upon the second coming of Jesus Christ. This group would have completely escaped from the sting of death!

The fourth festival is the Feast of Trumpets. This festival celebrates the "second coming of Jesus Christ" to intervene in world affairs, resurrect the first fruits, and establish the Kingdom of God on earth. This is a holy day. This is also where the "sheep" and "goats" separate as is referred to in Matthew 25:33–46.

The fifth festival is called the Day of Atonement. This is a festival which portrays the binding and removal of Satan for one-thousand years so that mankind at last may be made at one with God.

This is a holy day. This feast also pictures the atonement of up to half of the Laodiceanized Philadelphians during the great tribulation. Itso found reference to this atonement, in Matthew chapter 25:1-13.

The sixth festival is the Feast of Tabernacles. This feast represents the one-thousand-year rule of Christ and the Spirit-born children of God on earth, when salvation will be offered to all. The first day of this festival is therefore a holy day.

The seventh festival is known as the Last Great Day. It is a festival that pictures the Great White Throne judgment of Revelation 20:11. This festival is when the vast majority of humanity will be resurrected to mortal life and then they are given their opportunity for salvation. This is a holy day.

Bridging the Church Wheels of Time

THE WHEELS OF HEAVEN'S THRONE are mentioned in Ezekiel chapter 1. Itso had noticed that there were also wheels of time which moved through all seven festivals of God's human-salvation master plan.

Three of the seven festivals, the Pentecost, Trumpets, and Atonement, are also the third, fourth, and fifth festivals. It is these three festivals, Itso had noticed, that formed a bridge of time. This bridge separates the second Unleavened Bread Festival where salvation is not given to all, from the sixth Feast of Tabernacles festival. This tabernacles feast, is where by in this period of time, salvation will have been given to all.

From the Pentecost, Trumpets, and Atonement festivals, Itso could now begin to discern the workings of the Philadelphia Church of God as that of the sun, the moon, and of the stars. These are symbolically mentioned in the Bible as the true church of Revelation 12:1.

Latter-Day-Saint Mormons describe the workings of the Philadelphia generation or church, as the Celest (heaven), the Terrest (Paradise), and the Telest (Earth) kingdoms. The called of the Pentecost, the chosen of the Trumpets and the Faithful of the Atonement, point out the two witnesses of Philadelphia and the persecuted part of the church during the great tribulation period. See Revelation 17:14.

Nebuchadnezzar's Image versus the Handwriting on the Wall

ITSO HAD ALSO NOTICED THAT the four handwriting words of Daniel 5:25–28 had dovetailed beautifully with Nebuchadnezzar's image of Daniel 2:31–45. How would this be possible for Itso to even make a connection between what would seem to be two unrelated events?

By simply juxtapositioning the once repeated "number" of Daniel 5:25 onto the gold and silver of Nebuchadnezzar's image in chapter 2 verse 45. The balances of chapter 5 verse 27 would then therefore correspond to the "weight" of the brass and potter's clay together. The divided kingdom of chapter 5 and verse 28 would simply refer to the iron of Nebuchadnezzar's image in chapter 2 verse 45!

In terms of the church of Philadelphia, the gold represents the "transfigured" Philadelphians. Itso believes that these are the ones who have been translated from mortality to immortality and have thus escaped from death.

Next, is the silver part of the image. Itso believes that the silver, though not as shiny as the gold, represents all of those saints who have been resurrected from death itself. Though they have not escaped from "the valley of the shadow of death," as mentioned in Psalm 23:4, they are still resurrected into immortality to rule with Christ in his kingdom on earth.

Then comes the "balances" of conversion and repentance. This "potter's clay" of conversion has, within it, the consistency of both the brass of repentance and the silver of deliverance from death itself. It is good clay, which is easily bendable and moldable by the potter of Jesus Christ. These are the faithful mortals of Philadelphia who go through and survive the great tribulation itself!

Finally, there is the iron of unrepentant Laodiceans as well as the miry clay of unrepentant Philadelphians. The miry clay here does have the consistency of iron and dirt. It is therefore unmoldable and unshapeable by the master potter himself! All of this would therefore represent to Itso, the "division" that is found mentioned in both chapters of Daniel 2:41–43 and Daniel 5:28!

A Soldier Statue of Iron

ITSO HAD YET ANOTHER VISION. It was that of a terrifying soldier made from solid iron from head to feet.

This iron soldier was standing at full attention with his arms fully extended down the torso sides. His legs and feet were fully together down to the base of the terrible image that Itso could see.

The iron soldier image was also standing on land at what appeared to be one narrow end of a large rectangular pool of liquid water. The shape of this large rectangular pool was that which resembles a huge open doorway.

Itso had continued to observe the unfolding vision in front of him, as if it was on television. That is until the ground around the rectangular pool of water had begun to violently shake, like that of a huge earthquake. The previously calm and glass-like water of the rectangular pool was then also greatly agitated. The agitation of the water within the rectangular pool resembled a huge tidal tsunami.

A short space of what seemed to Itso like several minutes had passed by. The earth had continued to shake during this time, and the water in the rectangular pool had continued to be completely agitated.

That was when suddenly, there was a snapping sound at the base of the iron statue. The legs had completely separated at the statue's base where there were only the ankles, feet, and the ten toes which had remained.

Itso was truly amazed by what had happened next. The iron soldier statue with no feet had suddenly upended itself as it did a somersault head first directly into the watery-like rectangular pool.

By this action therefore, Itso had continued to witness until the iron statue had completely dissolved into the open doorway pool of acid-like water. Thereafter, did the tidal tsunami waves in the pool of water and the earth around the open-doorway pool had become both as smooth and as still like glass as they were before.

Only the iron feet and toes from the broken iron statue had remained intact on the ground beside the open-doorway pool of water. Itso could also see that there was absolutely nothing which had remained of the head, torso, and legs of the iron soldier that had plunged into the doorway pool. It had thus completely vanished forever, not to be seen again.

These are three similar bible verses that instantly come upon Itso's mind, in regard of his 'Soldier Statue of Iron' vision:

1) 'Behold, I have set before thee on open door, and no man can shut it.' (Rev. 3:8)
2) 'Death is swallowed up in victory.' (I Cor. 15:54), and
3) 'He will swallow up death in victory.' (Isa. 25:8)

What was Itso now to make of the iron soldier vision that he had witnessed? Was there any comparison to a similar vision that had occurred in the Bible? There most certainly was!

Iron Soldier versus Nebuchadnezzar's Image

At first glance, one would have to wonder whether there was any difference between Itso's Iron Soldier vision and Nebuchadnezzar's image. This image of Nebuchadnezzar is in reference to the biblical book of Daniel 2:31–45.

It was soon clear to Itso that these two distinct images, one of the iron soldier and the other of Nebuchadnezzar's dream image, had both represented two very notable and different time periods. The iron soldier vision of Itso is in fact the fulfillment of Daniel 2:40 of the Authorized King James Version: "And the fourth kingdom shall be as strong as iron: forasmuch as iron breaketh in pieces and subdueth (conquers) all things: and as iron that breaketh all these, shall it break in pieces and bruise."

Itso therefore believes that Daniel 2:40 marks the beginning of the great three-and-a-half years of tribulation. This is the beast mentioned in both chapters, thirteen and seventeen, in the book of Revelation! This is the Iron Soldier vision of Itso that is destined to come to world power to take place shortly before the great tribulation begins.

Thereafter is the time of "Jacob's Trouble," whereby Itso can now see the feet and ten toes remaining of the broken iron statue now consisting of both iron and clay. During this period of tribulation trouble, the Kingdom of Christ was set in place by means of the "Open Door" church of Philadelphia, which is mentioned in Revelation 3:7–8.

Itso had indeed noted about the two witnesses of Philadelphia, which are the "called" and the "chosen" ones who are now converted to immortality. These two witnesses are the "open" and "shut" doors which are found in Revelation 3:7.

Itso believes that God had specifically mentioned about the great tribulation period of Jacob's trouble with Daniel 2:41–43. During this short but intense period of trouble, Itso could now easily see differences and dividing lines here.

Differences and dividing lines during this terrible period include the unholy alliance between the shattered iron of verse 40 and the moist, miry clay. This unholy alliance is in total contrast to, and totally divided from, the molded potter's clay. The molded potter's clay refers to all of the atoned and converted mortal Philadelphians with the help of their two immortal witnesses who successfully survive the great tribulation trouble. They are thus mortally capable of populating Christ's millennium kingdom.

The terrible image of Nebuchadnezzar's dream comes to a dramatically sudden end at the end of the great tribulation period, or Jacob's trouble. This is when the "stone" of Jesus Christ's second coming collides with the iron and clay feet of the statue image, and thus, it is broken in pieces. Reference to this part of Nebuchadnezzar's image can be found in Daniel 2:34–35 as well as in verses 44–45.

Two Generational Cycles Times Five

As Itso has indicated already, there is a definite time difference between Itso's iron soldier image versus the gold, silver, bronze, iron, and clay image of King Nebuchadnezzar's dream. These two images therefore mark the boundary lines of which are both the beginning and ending of Jacob's great tribulation period. By usage of "generational cycles," Itso is able to further define the definite time periods which exist between these two materially different, but well-connected, statue images.

Itso had once again recalled Michael's statement just before Itso had exited the bus—"Got to go to sleep now," repeated once. The letter *o* is repeated five times. Letter *o* is the fifteenth letter of the twenty-six-letter alphabet. Thus, there are five of them of the alphabetical letter *o*. Due to the fact that the world economy goes through a complete cycle every fifteen years, Itso had simply multiplied fifteen years by five years, for a total of seventy-five years!

What Itso had forecasted her, is that in five economic cycles of fifteen years, from the end of World War II, will the great time of Jacob's trouble begin, with Itso's iron statue vision. When seventy-five years is added onto 1945, the year World War II ended, the number comes out to be the year of 2020!

Itso can even give a name to each fifteen-year economic cycle generation. All economic cycles are focused directly on the United States of America.

The 1945–1960 cycle is the "post-war" society. The 1960–1975 cycle is the "great" society. The 1975–1990 cycle is therefore the "post-great" society.

Not to mention also there is the "post–cold war" society, which had existed between the years of 1990 until the year of 2005. Itso now believes that the society for which we are living in now can be classified as the "pretribulation" society and is forecasted to end with the great tribulation which begins in 2020!

There are also five "political cycles." These are cycles of nineteen years each in length, for a total of ninety-five years. Each nineteen-year cycle does occur consecutively, and put together, the total time span for these five cycles does run from the year of 1929 to the year 2024!

Itso had therefore discovered that there is a four-year gap between the fifth economic cycle, which ends in the year 2020, and the fifth political cycle, which ends in the year of 2024. In Itso's estimation, this actually leaves more than enough time for the three-and-a-half-year great tribulation period!

From the stock-market crash in 1929 to the state of Israel creation in 1948 is political cycle one. Cycle two, with unification of Jerusalem under the Jews in 1967. Cycle three, with the Chernobyl nuclear disaster in 1986. Cycle four, with hurricane Katrina in 2005. Political cycle five would therefore come to an end in the year of 2024!

Convergence and Divergence Points of Cycles Fifteen and Nineteen

ITSO CAN ALSO LOCATE THE convergence and divergence points between both the fifteen-year economic cycle and the nineteen year political cycle. There is only one year, and one year only, by which Itso had noticed both the fifteen- and nineteen-year cycles as ending and beginning in the very same year. That one and only year of the convergence point of the fifteen- and nineteen- year cycles is in 2005!

The year 2005, as everyone remembers, brought the passing away of Pope John Paul II. Hurricane Katrina had also struck along the U.S. Gulf Coast and the city of New Orleans. Some of what remains of King David's palace was also unearthed in 2005 near Jerusalem in Israel.

Greater convergence points of the consecutive economic and political cycles have also been discovered by Itso. These include the five economic cycles of fifteen years each which did begin in 1930 and ended in 2005. This also is another seventy-five-year period.

The political cycle of 1929 to 1948, therefore, runs roughly concurrent to the 1930 to 1945 economic cycle. This is the very economic cycle which has marked the great depression and that of World War II! By the very divergence points of cycles fifteen and nineteen is one able to calculate the length of the great tribulation period. It is between the year 2020 and 2024.

Other Generational Cycles

ITSO HAS COME TO ACCEPT the possibility that there are other seventy-year generational cycles beyond that of the three diasporic seventy-year cycles already mentioned. Especially so from the ending of the third diasporic cycle of 1844 to 1914. Itso then had calculated yet another seventy-year generational cycle between the years of 1914 to 1984.

Recall as well that it was Itso in 1984 who had a conversation with Michael on the bus. As a part of the conversation. Michael had said to Itso, "I was born on the second of August, 1950." Itso had previously wondered before about the meaning of this.

It was not until many years later did Itso come to the realization that "August 2, 1950," could very well have been the beginning of the final seventy-year generation before the sudden outbreak of Jacob's trouble. With the addition of seventy years onto that of August 2, 1950, Itso again had the exact year of the great tribulation's beginning as that of 2020!

Itso believes now that the conversation he had with Michael on the bus in 1984 had also marked the beginning of the final forty-year-judgment cycle. This is a forty-year cycle that includes the great tribulation period.

Jacob's trouble thereafter ends in 2024, the year Christ comes back to proclaim the millennium and to also defeat Satan. Must as the ancient Israelites had to wait for forty years to enter the promised land of Canaan due to rebellion, the latter-day Philadelphians must also wait forty years for Christ to proclaim his kingdom in 2024!

Last Judgment Cycle and Great Tribulation

Itso is also now aware of the distinctly concurrent connection between the last judgment cycle of forty-years and the great tribulation of Jacob's trouble. This period of great trouble appears for Itso to occupy the final four years of the judgment cycle concurrently between 2020 and 2024!

What is Itso now to make of the final paragraph that pertains to the Mystery of Civilization, chapter 4 in Herbert W. Armstrong's publication of *Mystery of the Ages*? The final paragraph in this particular chapter states, "These are the very last days of Satan's evil world. God's utopian civilization will be started with the present generation."

Itso now had to be completely aware of the two sentences which do form the final but short paragraph at the end of the fourth chapter. These two sentences in the paragraph had thus caused Itso to ask some basic questions about the period which will lead to the Millennial Kingdom:

1) Do "the very last days" of sentence one refer to the forty-year judgement cycle before the millennium?
2) Will "God's utopian civilization" of sentence two be also in reference to the great tribulation period of Jacob's trouble?

Temple Code Solved

It is essential for Itso to understand the interplay which happens to go on between the literal and allegorical methods that are involved in the ability to therefore solve the *temple code*. Without the definite starting and ending points of which the temple code itself does provide, it can be impossible for Itso to understand and to solve the temple code by any natural means. The temple code itself is therefore a supernatural code by its very existence and by its very origin!

The temple code itself is also compatible with, and is comparable to, the Bible code. As the Bible itself is fully able to explain its own prophetic symbolism, Itso believes that the temple code is also able to explain its own prophetic symbolism complementary to the Bible.

Following, is displayed the entire temple code as it first appears in its unsolved and natural state:

1) Saloon Nuts;
2) Pitted Sunflower Seeds;
3) Got to go to sleep now;
4) Got to go to sleep now.

All of the entire temple code is now compared with Itso's upended Iron Statue vision, Nebuchadnezzar's dream image, and the handwriting on the wall of Daniel chapter 5:25–28. The results are as follows:

1) Saloon Nuts=Legs=Division=Iron
2) Pitted Sunflower Seeds=Waist=Weight=Potter's Clay and Bronze

117

3) Got to go to sleep now=Arms and Chest=Number=Silver
4) Got to go to sleep now=Head=Number=Gold

Drop all five *s*'s in points one and two, then drop all five *o*'s in points three and four.

The temple code now looks like this:

1) aloon nut
2) pitted unflower eed
3) gttgt sleep nw
4) gttgt sleep nw

Fully interpreted, the temple code now looks like this:

1) aloon nut=antichrist rule
2) pitted unflower eed=
   a) Pentagon (or people) in tidal tsunami-earthquake destruction
   b) United Nations (building) found (or founded 1945), lower earthquake damage

3) gttgt sleep nw=
   a) great tidal tsunami generated
   b) total slaughter, earthquake, people
   c) New York (City), Washington (DC)

4) gttgt sleep nw=
   a) giant tidal tsunami generated
   b) terrible slaughter
   c) English earthquake
   d) Pentagon, nuclear war.

The Reign of Antichrist

It is that Itso had proceeded to solve the temple code entirely with the help of the Holy Spirit. Itso could now see the sequence of timed events in the entire reign of antichrist, from its beginning, all the way to the finish, as close to seven years in length. The middle of antichrist reign of seven years, is therefore interrupted by a major nuclear war.

Itso could already foresee that there has been a double fulfillment, symbolic and literal, of prophecies which pertain to both the lesser and the greater tribulation periods of the antichrist rule. The lesser part of the seven-year tribulation span, Itso believes, is the 1,290-day period of Daniel 12:11.

An interlude of a forty-five-day nuclear war in Daniel 12:12 is what does precede the greater tribulation. It is an interlude which does divide the lesser part from the greater part of the tribulation itself.

The greater part of the tribulation period is what Itso believes as the three-and-a-half year, 1,260 days that precedes the start of the one-thousand-year millennium of Jesus Christ. References to this period of time, that of the greater tribulation, are found in Daniel 12:7 and in Revelation 13:5.

There had been certainly a seventy-year generational countdown to the beginning of the 1,260-day "greater tribulation" period. This is a countdown as has been previously mentioned, which began on August 2, 1950 and would end on August 2, 2020.

The calendar date of August 2, 2020, is what Itso could point to as to when the greater tribulation period begins. The great tribulation would end in the year of 2024, or 1,260 days later, as the Millennial Kingdom had dawned.

Reference to both the lesser and greater periods of antichrist rule is mentioned in Revelation 17:11. It says, "And the beast that was, and is not, Even he is the eighth, and is of the seven, and goeth into perdition [destruction]."

Itso then asked the question: "Who are the 'blessed' from God's point of view?"

This was indeed a question now, which was important for Itso to ask. There are two clearly stated verses in the Bible that are focused upon exactly who the "blessed" of Daniel chapter 12 really are.

The first of the two verses that Itso discovered are from Daniel 12:11, which says, "And from the time that the daily sacrifice shall be abolished, and the abomination [the king of the north] that maketh desolate set up, there shall be a thousand two-hundred and ninety days."

Itso does happen to believe that the "daily sacrifice" of verse eleven above is the prayer of "daily Sabbath remembrance," and that being none other than the Lord's prayer of Matthew 6:9–13. Itso thus can believe also that the Lord's prayer does come with the fourth Bible commandment of Exodus 20:8, which says, 'Remember the Sabbath day to keep it holy."

It is also a period of 1,290 days, of which Itso believes, to be and is a very rough time for the Philadelphia level ones. The level ones are those destined to be raptured into heaven. That said, however, Itso believes that all is not lost upon the earth.

In the second verse, Daniel 12:12, it says, "Blessed is he that waiteth, and [he that] cometh to the [end of the] thousand three-hundred and five and thirty days."

Itso believes, therefore, that the "he that waiteth" in the above second Daniel verse, does in fact refer to the Philadelphia level ones who are successfully raptured into the kingdom of heaven. This is the rapture period of three-days which Itso believes comes immediately after (the level ones) 1,290-day trial period on the earth. See also Revelation 3:10.

It is the part of Daniel 12:12 that says, "And cometh to the thousand three-hundred and five and thirty days," that Itso also finds to be the most interesting. Here is where it appears that there is another group of Philadelphians that are mentioned, those in level three.

Itso believes that level three Philadelphians would have witnessed both the rapture of the level ones and the resurrection of the level twos.

Itso therefore believes that some of the Philadelphia threes are to survive World War III. This is a war which is due to erupt suddenly during the forty-five-day period between the 1,290 and the 1,335 days.

Surviving Philadelphia threes, Itso believes, are thereafter selected by God to help and construct the third Jewish Temple during the Great Tribulation aftermath of 1,260 days. More about this time period of "great tribulation" is found in the "temple" chapter of Revelation 11 in the King James Bible.

Itso's earlier mention of the striking similarities in people of any symptoms between Volcanic Radiation Sickness (VRS) and Nuclear Radiation Sickness (NRS) should no longer even be of any surprise. Either way, Itso believes that different plagues and diseases, whether they be new or old, are thus and therefore the natural outcomes of both volcanic and nuclear radiation sicknesses!

The point Itso now makes here is that while the effects of VRS can never be cancelled out by the effects of NRS, it is God in heaven who will never allow for the complete and total extinction of the human race on earth in any case. A very careful study of both Revelation 11 and Psalm 91 will make this point absolutely clear.

Itso does believe, therefore, that the coming VRS-NRS pandemic will soon sweep the entire globe within a short period of the next few years. As of late summer in 2014, Itso has some five general questions to ask in regards to the VRS-NRS pandemic:

1) Is modern airline travel the means by which the VRS pandemic is spread throughout the entire globe? Daniel 12:4 says that "many shall run to and fro, and knowledge shall be increased."

2) Would an Islamist takeover of Ethiopia, as well as the beginning decline of global population, allow for the anti-

christ to be in full charge of Europe by sometime during 1,335 days?

3) Will the VRS pandemic, therefore, decimate about 45–50 percent of the global population in 1,290 days, from December of 2016 to the middle of June in 2020?

4) Will the following nuclear war in July of 2020 further reduce the world's global population by another 40–45 percent?

5) In the following nuclear aftermath and great tribulation period of 1,260 days, will there instantly be enough level three, mortal Philadelphians available to construct the third Jewish Temple, as in 144,000?

So when, therefore, during the seven-year tribulation period, is the Philadelphia church to be raptured, or evacuated, into the Kingdom of Heaven for its own safety? thought Itso. *Will the church be entirely evacuated from the beginning of, or in the middle of, or at the very end of the seven-year tribulation period?*

There never was any sense to Itso for the church evacuation to occur at the end of year seven of the tribulation, just when the thousand-year millennium had dawned. For many years, Itso had wrestled with the question as to whether the church evacuation would occur either at the beginning or in the middle of the tribulation period!

Not until August 3, 2015, did the Holy Spirit reveal the true answer to Itso about the tribulation rapture. The answer: both. Both, at the beginning and the middle of the seven-year tribulation period.

Well, how could the church rapture occur twice? Isn't there, then, to occur only one church rapture either at the beginning of the tribulation or in the middle of the tribulation period? Which is it? thought Itso.

The answer, once again, is both. Daniel 12:11 says, "There shall be a thousand two-hundred and ninety days." This number of days is the opening phase of the seven-year tribulation period. Itso believes that this opening phase of 1,290 days is also known as the Feast of Pentecost.

God, therefore, gives plenty of time, 1,290 days, to evacuate the church into heaven before the forty-five day nuclear-war period, or Feast of Trumpets, begins. In the aftermath of nuclear war, or the Feast of Atonement, is when the third Jewish Temple shall be constructed.

Itso believes this is the very temple that antichrist will temporarily occupy but shall be permanently usurped by Jesus Christ at the end of 1260 days! Please see 2 Thessalonians 2:4.

In Revelation 11:9, it says, "And they of the people and kindreds and tongues and nations shall see their dead bodies three days and a half, and shall not suffer their dead bodies to be put into graves."

Itso believes that this verse refers directly to the two witnesses of the rapture and that of the resurrection. The rapture and resurrection had occurred by this time, already, so no graves are now open to those two prophets. See Revelation 11:10.

In Revelation 11:11–12 is where 144,000 temple builders now placed in the wilderness will be evacuated into heaven at the end of the 1,260-day great tribulation. The 144,000 temple builders are not, and should not, be confused with the previous two prophets, or witnesses, who were evacuated after 1,290 days! See Daniel 12:12.

Itso now believes that the Lord God does bring a Roman coin from the fish's mouth and Jonah from the whale's mouth after three days (Jonah 1:17; 2:10). What all of this means to Itso is that God will allow his third Jewish Temple to be constructed, which does indeed set the stage for the thousand-year millennium to finally begin.

Now Itso can see that Daniel 12:7–13 does mention the precise number of days that must surely come to pass before the millennium itself will really begin. In Daniel 12:7, the Feast of Atonement is in progress. This atonement, therefore, includes the construction of the third Jewish temple! Two other feasts, that of the Pentecost (1,290 days) and that of trumpets (45 days), have by then been completed and thus, are now have become the two witnesses of the book of Revelation.

The countdown number of days to the millennium's start, therefore, is a total of 2,595 days. This is a timespan of seven years. This is also a timeline that Itso can see, as literal number of days countdown to the beginning of the millennium!

When Itso had used the very reference point of August 2, 1950, he simply counted forward by seventy years to the year of 2020. Itso then counted backward in time, from August 2, 2020, by a span of 1,335 days. The result?

1) "Former Cuban leader Fidel Castro, burial December 4, 2016."
2) "The church rapture to last for 1,290 days?"
3) "Will Germany itself fall to Islam during this time?"

Summer and Winter Solstices

IN REGARD TO THE SUMMER solstice, Itso had found that the King James Version of the Holy Bible has this to say in Matthew 23:32–33: "Now learn a parable of the fig tree; When his branch is yet tender, and putteth forth leaves, ye know that summer is nigh; So likewise ye, when ye shall see all these things, know that it is near, even at the doors."

Itso had now some further questions, and they pertain to the above-mentioned verses (32–33):

1) Shall see all what things?
2) The rapture and resurrection of the church?
3) Know what is near?
4) The Great Tribulation?
5) Even at what doors?
6) The doors of the summer and winter solstices?

In regard to the winter solstice, Itso discovered that the King James Version of the Holy Bible, also in Matthew 24:20–21: "But pray ye that your flight be not in the winter, neither on the Sabbath day: For then shall be great tribulation, Such as was not since the beginning of the world to this time, no, nor ever shall be."

Itso had now some further questions, and they pertain to the above-mentioned verses (20–21):

1) Verse 20 refer to summer solstice beginning of the Great Tribulation?

2) The Sabbath day refer to Christ's Second Advent at the end of the Great Tribulation?

So how would there be a possible numerical connection between the summer and the winter solstices? Itso wondered.

The answer to this connection, in Itso's opinion, would be in the length of time in which the antichrist, or "beast," would rule upon the earth. The book of Revelation 13:4–5 have this to say: "And they worshipped the dragon which gave power unto the beast: and they worshipped the beast, saying; Who is like unto the beast? Who is able to make war with him? And there was given unto him a mouth speaking great things and blasphemies: and power was given unto him to continue forty and two months."

Itso did discover in verse 5 that the "forty and two months" does translate into three-and-a-half years, or three times twelve, plus six months. It also says in verse 5, "and power was given unto him to continue forty and two months." This part of verse 5 indicates to Itso that the beast had previously risen to power for a certain period of time before given power to continue. All that Itso can say at this point is that the family of righteousness has triumphed over the family of evil, in Itso's estimation, as surely as death is swallowed-up in victory!

Any point to any parallel numbers that had existed between the two solstices, of summer and winter? thought Itso.

Itso also had wondered whether there would thus be a connection between the reign of the antichrist and the Temple Mount in Jerusalem. Itso had now decided to look into and to then consider that this is a very possible likelihood!

Itso does believe that God had prophesied, through the prophet Nathan, to King David of Israel about a future third Jewish temple to yet be built. This is a Bible prophecy revealed in 1 Chronicles 17:10–14: "I declare to you that the Lord will build a house for you: When your days are over and you go to be with your ancestors, I will raise up your offspring to succeed you, one of your own sons, and I will establish his Kingdom. He is the one who will build a house for me, and I will establish his throne forever. I will be his father, and he will be my son. I will never take my love away from him, as I took it away from your predecessor. I will set him over my house and my Kingdom forever; his throne will be established forever."

It was, therefore, when the Lord God had finished his prophecy, that Nathan, in verse 15, reported to David all that was said by the Lord God. What a truly remarkable prophecy this is!

To be able to even think that Jesus Christ will be able to raise and assemble 144,000 builders of the temple! Itso has discovered this 1 Chronicles prophecy to be in exact accordance with verses in Revelation 7:11 and 14!

Chapter 5

The Great Historical Beyond

The Temple Mount

ITSO'S PARENTAL FATHER WAS ON United Nations peace-keeping duties in the Middle-Eastern conflict zone during the 1964 to 1965 period. Itso's father had lots of stories to tell along with the mostly black-and-white photographs that he had brought back with him.

These were black-and-white photos which had revealed some of the major landmarks and tourist destinations in both Egypt and in Israel. A few of the photographs, which Itso had recalled he saw, were that of King Tutankhamen's tomb in Egypt's "Valley of the Kings," King Tutankhamen's golden sarcophagus in the Cairo museum, and of the "Dome of the Rock" Muslim shrine located in the older part of Jerusalem.

Itso had now turned to the 1995 edition of *The New Encyclopedia Britannica*, where it says that:

1) "The Dome of the Rock in Jerusalem, was built between A.D. six-hundred eighty-five and six-hundred ninetyone by the caliph 'Abd al-Malik ibn Marwan, not as a mosque for public worship but rather as a 'mashhad,' a shrine for pilgrims."
2) "It is virtually the first monumental building in Islamic history and is of considerable aesthetic and architectural importance."

Encyclopedia Britannica, Itso noted, says also that the "Mosque of Omar" shrine in Jerusalem, or the Arabic "Qubbat Assakhrah," is the "oldest extant Islamic monument."

It says also that "the rock over which the shrine was built is sacred to both Muslims and Jews." And that "The Prophet Muhammed, founder of Islam, is traditionally believed to have ascended into heaven from the site."

Gage Canadian and *Webster's* dictionaries both indicate to Itso the year of 632 AD as the exact year of the prophet Muhammed's death. Itso was very interested to take particular notice in the study of the Bible book of Daniel 12:11–12.

In the King James Version of Daniel 12:11, Itso had noticed that it says, "And from the time 'that' the daily 'sacrifice' shall be taken away, and the abomination that maketh desolate set up 'there shall be' a thousand two-hundred and ninety days."

In Daniel 12:12, Itso had then discovered that it says, "Blessed 'is' he that waiteth, and commeth to the thousand three-hundred and five and thirty days."

Itso had noticed here that in the number of days mentioned in verses 11 and 12, there is a gap of fortyfive days. With an application of the "day for a year" principle, those forty-five days then become forty-five years. Itso had now applied this same principle to the total number of days that Itso did see mentioned in verse 11 and in verse 12. To Itso, this day for a year substitution now really begins to become interesting!

From the Arab-Israeli conflict of 1967, Itso just simply counted backward in time, as he has used the 1335 days or years as mentioned in Daniel 12:12. This takes Itso to exactly 632 AD! This is the year whereby in accordance to *Encyclopedia Britannica*, the Islamic founder Muhammed had ascended to heaven from the Jewish temple mount. That is the same temple mount which was abandoned by the Roman army after they had destroyed the second Jewish temple in 70 AD!

Now here is where Itso had found that the forty-five days' worth of years can be calculated for the purpose of both an observation forward and backward in time. Itso began with the year of 1967, when Itso had his first visions of God. Itso had simply subtracted forty-five years from 1967. This subtraction had now taken Itso to the year of 1922. The year 1922 was the same year as Howard Carter's discovery of none other than King Tutankhamen's tomb in that part of Egypt, known as the "Valley of the Kings."

Another fulfillment of Daniel's 1,290 days had Itso discovered. With the addition from the year that Mohammed had ascended to heaven in 632 AD, of 1,290 days, or years, the total sum of 1,922 days or years is now reached.

An addition of the extra forty-five days does indeed allow for Daniel's 1,335 days of chapter 12 verse 12 to be therefore directly in line with the year of 1967. The year 1967, as everyone should know by now, was the year in which the Jews had unified the city of Jerusalem in the six-day war fought against the Arabs.

Is this then another indication of Jesus Christ's second coming upon the face of the earth? thought Itso.

From the year of the death and recorded ascension of the Prophet Muhammed into heaven, Itso's addition of forty-five days, or years, onto 632 AD would result in the year of 677 AD! Itso, though, did not find anything of major historical significance to have taken place in that year. However, *Encyclopedia Britannica* had mentioned that when construction of the Dome of the Rock shrine in Jerusalem had been underway, as between the years of 685–691 AD. It would there-fore seem to be perfectly logical in Itso's view that a certain period of time would have to have taken place for plans to build the shrine to be available even before the construction of it would actually begin!

Itso had now moved forward in time, by 1,290 years from when plans of the shrine had supposedly began in 677 AD. This, therefore, would bring Itso back again to the year of 1967.

Forty-five day-years, Itso believes, is actually a duo proph-ecy fulfillment about the actual reign of the beast upon the temple mount in Jerusalem during and after a major nuclear war. This forty-five-day prophecy, found in Daniel 12:12, can also be rendered in line with the Maya-Hopi calendar date of December 21, 2012, when forty-five day-years is added onto the year of 1967!

Television images viewed by Itso had revealed that the Mount of Olives is in visual range of the temple mount of old Jerusalem and also of the Dome of the Rock shrine, which is also situated atop of the temple mount.

In the Old Testament Bible book of Zechariah 14:4, in the King James Version, Itso had read an interesting statement by which he deems to be prophetic: "And his feet shall stand in that day upon the Mount of Olives, which is' before Jerusalem on the east, and the Mount of Olives shall cleave in the midst thereof toward the east and toward the west, 'and there shall be' a very great valley; and half of the mountain shall remove toward the north, and half of it toward the south."

Many questions, Itso now had to ask, when he had read the Bible statement about Zechariah 14:4:

1) Is there a total rapture or transfiguration of part of the church in 2020?

2) A total resurrection of the other half of the church, beginning three days later, in 2020?

3) Christ to build his church in three days, symbolic of the prophet Jonah in the whale's belly for three days?

4) Does the resurrection begins when Christ thereby touches his feet upon the Mount of Olives near Jerusalem, which produces a massive earthquake and splits the mount in two?

5) Is the Dome of the Rock, the third holiest shrine in all of Islam, and in visual sight of the Mount of Olives, to be destroyed by this massive earthquake?

6) Are shockwaves, which result from the massive earthquake, to be severely felt everywhere worldwide?

7) Is the battle of Armageddon in the year 2024 and Christ's proclamation of the millennium kingdom and white throne judgement?

The grave political implications of the great tribulation and the second coming of Jesus Christ upon the Mount of Olives can only be possibly barely imagined at best! thought Itso.

In Itso's opinion, Christ's great tribulation and Second Advent do bring us forward to and past the late spring to early summer solstice of June 21, 2020. It is also the time, Itso believes, when a nuclear battle in the Middle East shall begin. Itso's basis for this solemn forecast is in verse 7 of Daniel chapter 12: "That 'it shall be' for a time, times, and an half."

Further questions of which Itso had that concerns Daniel 12:7:

1) A half time, when the antichrist consolidates his power after a twenty-seven-day nuclear war, of which is mentioned by the seer Nostradamus?
2) Times during which a third Jewish temple is to be built?
3) A time during which is initiated the final battle of Armageddon?

Not all is lost upon Itso. In particular are two Bible verses from 2 Thessalonians chapter 2. From the New Testament, the Gideon's version, Itso had found verses 3 and 4 to be the most interesting. Verse 3 says, "Let no one in any way deceive you, for it will not come unless the apostasy comes first, and the man of lawlessness is revealed, the son of destruction."

Questions about verse 3 that had now come upon Itso's mind include:

1) The phrase "it will not come" in reference to the resurrection of the church into heaven and the great tribulation thereafter?
2) The apostasy in reference to the fall away from the faith?
3) The man of lawlessness who is revealed, the son of destruction, the antichrist? The fourth horse of the apocalypse?

When Itso had now begun to study verse 4, Itso had found that it says, "Who opposes and exalts himself above every so-called god or object of worship, so that he takes his seat in the temple of God displaying himself as being God."

Questions about verse 4 that also now come upon the mind of Itso in addition to those questions of verse 3:

1) Is the "temple of God" mentioned in verse 4 referring to the third Jewish Temple which is to be built where the temple mount in Jerusalem now stands presently?

2) Will the entering into this temple by the antichrist be what triggers the Armageddon battle of 2023–4?

3) Will the political intrigue existing between the king of the north (antichrist?), and the king of the south (false prophet?), as is mentioned in the eleventh chapter of Daniel, appear to be resolved by a false peace treaty?

4) Will this false peace treaty result in the consolidation of the antichrist's power and the construction of the third Jewish Temple?

5) Will the decree or edict to construct this third Jewish Temple be given by the antichrist on precisely the winter solstice date of December 21, 2020?

6) Will the breaking of this false peace treaty by the antichrist result in the final battle in the valley of Megiddo located north of Jerusalem? This is where Itso believes that the battle of Armageddon happens to originate.

So that Itso could obtain a proper view of future occurrences, Itso had found that it is equally important to have proper insight for what also had occurred in the past. This level of insight was a matter most important. It was a past insight also brought to Itso's attention by the Holy Spirit.

Heavens or Heaven?

THERE HAD TO BE TWO understandings, Itso believes, behind Genesis 1:1. Some versions of English-speaking Bibles have as their first verse, "God created the heavens." In the original authorized King James Version, it says, "In the beginning, God created the heaven and the earth."

How deeply rich in meaning has Itso found these words! To bring alone this one verse at the start of Genesis into a better understanding, in Itso's opinion, gives it an entirely new and different appreciation:

> "In the beginning [Christ] God [by the Holy Spirit] created the [kingdom of] heaven [with its Holy Angels] and the earth [Universal Void, with its fallen angels]" (v. 1)

When Itso had read the second verse of Genesis chapter one, Itso did find a wonderful connection that the second verse really has with the very first verse. In the second verse, it clearly states that the "planetary system" at this point had yet to be formed within the earth-void.

The "big bang" of planets to yet occur from this point? Itso wondered.

"And the earth was without form, and void; and darkness 'was' [fallen angels were] upon the face [planetary orbs] of the deep [universe]" (v.2).

And the Spirit of God moved upon the face (planetary orbs) of the waters (angels). Itso now believes, thus, that the next three verses of Genesis—verses 3, 4, and 5 therefore talks about God's progressive separation of the holy angels from the fallen angels. It is when Itso had read the sixth verse of Genesis chapter 1 that Itso now believes that God begins to mention any possibility of a planetary system of expanse which fills the entire universal earth-void. This planetary expanse, Itso believes, would be at the very beginning of the second day of creation!

"And God said, Let there be a firmament [planetary system] in the midst of the waters [angels], and let it divide the waters [fallen angels] from the waters [holy angels]" (v. 6).

Verse number 7 of Genesis that follows, therefore, is thus a further clarification from verse 6 of Genesis. This clearly indicates to Itso that before God even begins to act upon the angelic realm, he first pronounces his judgement upon that very realm!

"And God made the firmament [planetary system] and divided the waters [fallen angels] which were under the firmament [planetary system of heaven] from the waters [holy angels] which were above the firmament [planetary-system in heaven]: and it was so" (v.7).

Now upon Itso's reading of the eighth verse of Genesis chapter 1, Itso had found it a bit strange at first for God to name the firmament which God had created, "heaven." Strange that is, until Itso had come to the realization that the individual planets which "are" the firmament within the universal earth-void are all globular in shape.

What these globular shapes of all the planets in the universe therefore tells Itso is that they are all a reflection although an imperfect reflection of none other than the mom of all planets, the Kingdom of Heaven! If there are any lingering doubts about the true appearance of the Kingdom of Heaven, then Itso had let these doubts be quickly driven away by Itso's reading Psalm 119:105: "Thy word [Holy Spirit] is a lamp [planetary firmament] unto my feet, and a light [way] unto my path [body of existence].

Itso believes, therefore, that the word of God, as its own existence of the Holy Spirit, is both a lamp, which is a material object, and a light, which is a spiritual object. Itso believes also that both lamp and light are in perfect balance and are thus in harmony with each other, just as the physical material bodies of holy angels are in perfect balance with their spiritual bodies. There is no difference, Itso believes, between these two, the material and the spiritual bodies. Put together, both aspects of the physical and material body exist in immortality.

In the Kingdom of Heaven, therefore, Itso believes that in other words, there is no difference between these two bodies, which are the material and the spiritual. One body is merely an extension of the other!

Other more modern versions of the Bible, Itso had noticed, have in them, "God created the heavens," instead of "God created the heaven," as part of their chapter 1, verse 1 in Genesis. Itso's view about having an extra *s* added onto Genesis 1:1 is that this is not really necessary. Not only is an extra *s* not necessary in Itso's opinion, but it is also confusing.

"Why and how," Itso would ask, "could the mere addition of a single *s* onto the word *heaven* in Genesis chapter 1 verse 1 be even so confusing?"

It is confusing because Itso believes that in the first verse of Genesis, a singular *heaven*, means the Kingdom of Heaven; while a pluralized heaven, with the added *s*, means the system of planets! It therefore makes absolutely no sense, in Itso's opinion, for God to say in Genesis 1:1 that he, God, "created the heavens and the earth," or system of planets when it was not until the sixth verse of Genesis chapter 1 that he, God, had allowed a "firmament" to be created!

By the time that Itso does manage to read the first verse of the second chapter of Genesis, Itso finds no problem with the pluralized heaven here. This is because of "the firmament" that was mentioned before when Itso had read back to Genesis 1:7!

"You cannot have it both ways," was Itso's opinion. "It is either that you believe the singular, creationist model of 'heaven,' mentioned in Genesis one verse one, and therefore the Kingdom of Heaven, or instead of this, is the evolutionary model of 'heavens' in Genesis one verse one, which conveniently does deny the very existence of the Kingdom of Heaven!"

So which is it then? was Itso's next thought. *Does evolution come before creation, as in "heavens," or does creation come before evolution, as in "heaven?"*

Angels to Fallen Angels

SOMETIME AGO, ITSO DID COME across a manufactured plastic wall ornament of Itso's natural parental mother's possession. It was a wall ornament which did consist of a fancy, silvery lace-like trim around its circumference, whose size resembled that of a small plate. At the center of this brown-colored plate, there contained some fancy silver words lettered in the German language. Not so fluent in German, Itso had asked his mother one day for its equivalent English translation.

"In wine lies the truth," Itso's mother had said to him.

My, oh my, thought Itso. *What fundamental truth does the wine belie?*

Safe to say at this point and any dictionary will tell Itso exactly what is the very definition of wine. In simple terms, it is the fermented grape juice, which by its fermentation has turned into alcohol.

Of course, Itso knows that there are other foods as well that ferment and turn into alcohol such as the turning of wheat into beer. Now then, if Itso was given a choice between the drinking of pure grape juice or wine, Itso would rather be drinking the pure grape juice each and every time. In Itso's opinion, grape juice tastes better than wine.

Personally, Itso is quite confident that God Almighty in heaven would know the difference between the pure grape juice and the corrupted grape juice that we know as wine. Examples of this fundamental truth, Itso believes, do abound in the word of God, and this also most certainly includes the Bible itself.

Itso has only to look at the driving statistics on our roadways today to understand the truth behind the Bible book of Proverbs

20:1. In the King James Version of the Bible, Proverbs 20:1 says, "Wine is a mocker, strong drink is raging; and whosoever is deceived thereby is not wise."

Itso might now ask, "How could one be possibly deceived by the wine?"

Itso had next let Proverbs 23:29–35 put away any notion or idea that you cannot be deceived. This is what Itso believes that verses 29 and 30 has to say about the deception of wine: "Who hath woe? who hath sorrow? who hath contentions? who hath babbling? who hath wounds without cause? who hath redness of eyes? They that tarry long at the wine, they that go to seek mixed wine."

The inevitable result of too much wine is entirely predictable for Itso to see. No tricks, lies, or deceptions here. The last verse in Proverbs 23, is where verse 35 says, "They have stricken me, 'shalt thou say, and' I was not sick; they have beaten me, 'and' I felt it not: when shall I awake? I will seek it yet again."

Itso now had some very deep questions in regards to Proverbs 23:35:

1) Does verse 35 not sound like the modern-day alcoholic addiction which some people are experiencing today? How well does this addiction continue to influence our natural behavior as much today as it did in ancient times!

2) One's eyes looking at strange women and one's heart saying some bad things lately in accordance with Proverbs 23:33?

How about Noah, patriarch of the flood, whom Itso discovered had exhibited some post-flood bad behavior when he planted a vineyard? Genesis 9:21 says, "And he drank of the wine, and was drunken: and he was uncovered within his tent."

Two of Noah's sons, Shem and Japeth, had taken a garment and covered their father's nakedness (Gen. 9:23). The damage was already done to its youngest son, Ham, father of Canaan, who had earlier seen his father's nakedness (Gen. 9:22). Itso believes that Noah's nakedness was only one example of how wine alone had influenced the world's generations right down to this day.

Another memorable example that Itso believes of good wine versus bad wine in the Bible, King James Version, would have to be at the wedding in Cana of Galilee. This marriage was recorded in the gospel book of John 2:1–11.

Itso had read in verse three that when the wedding party guests were out of wine, Jesus's mother went to him saying so. Jesus then replied to his mother in verse 4, "Woman, what have I to do with thee? Mine hour is not come."

Now is it possible, Itso had wondered that as bridegroom, *"mine hour is not come" is in reference to both Jesus's imminent wedding to his girlfriend, Mary Magdalene, in Cana and his later last supper with Jesus's disciples which does point to Jesus's imminent crucifixion?*

There are other places of which Itso had discovered in the gospel book of John where Mary Magdalene could also be mentioned. These places would include Jesus talking with a woman of Samaria, by Jacob's well (John 4:1–42); The adulterous woman (John 8:3–11); Mary and her sister Martha (John 11:1–2); Mary anointing Jesus's feet (John 12:3); Mary Magdalene by the cross of Jesus (John 19:25); and Mary Magdalene who was by the tomb of Jesus (John 20:1–18).

It is possible, in Itso's estimation, that the ruler and governor of the Cana feast, of whom Itso had assumed to be the rabbi, upon tasting the water turned into wine, in verse 9 of John chapter 2, did not even know of where this wine had come from. Itso does believe that the feast's manager obviously had nevertheless known the difference between good wine and bad wine as Itso could see from verse 10. Here is where Itso believes that the ruler of the feast may have known as to when the good wine would be normally gone but did not know that it was Christ the bridegroom who had manufactured the best wine of all!

You think it must have been grape juice that Jesus made? I think so, Itso thought.

Itso would have guessed by now that the making of grape juice and wine would have gone back to a long way in history. How far back in history, Itso might say? Well, all of the way back to the Kingdom of Heaven to be absolutely sure.

Frankly speaking, Itso had strongly suspected that God had always a strong preference for grape -juice instead of wine. So much so, in fact, that God had commanded his entire angelic realm in heaven to neither produce wine nor to drink any wine whatsoever.

Did any of God's six-hundred million angels obey God on the matter of not drinking any wine? Well, Itso had correctly guessed that two-thirds, or four-hundred million angels, were wise enough to obey God about not drinking wine.

The other two-hundred million angels, not so much. Talk about the fallen angel's own murder by wine, then women, and then by song! More like suicide by disobedience, if you really want to ask Itso!

Itso had turned next to where Jesus spoke a parable. It is mentioned in both the book of Mark 12:1–11 and in Luke 20:9–18. It is a parable which begins with the words: "A 'certain' man planted a vineyard."

With these opening words of Mark 12 and in Luke 20:9, there was now some questions asked by Itso:

1) Is this 'certain' man, God the Father, who had put the hedge (heaven) around the vineyard (universe)?
2) The place he dug for the winevat, Babylon?
3) The tower he built in the midst of it, Zion or the New Jerusalem?
4) The husbandmen for which he let it (Babylon) out to, fallen angels?
5) The far country that he went into for a long time, the Kingdom of Heaven?

Itso had also read that at different times, God sent four servants to his vineyard. All were caught, beaten, sent away empty, wounded, severely injured, and killed.

1) The first and last (fourth) servant of the vineyard, Jesus Christ Himself?
2) The second servant of the vineyard, Enoch, who walked with God (Gen. 5:24)?

3) The third servant, Noah, of none other than the great flood (Gen. 6:17)?
4) What inevitably happens, as is mentioned in Mark 12:9 and in Luke 20:16?
5) The husbandmen (fallen angels) are destroyed, and the vineyard is given away to others?

The devil in charge of the wine, it seems to Itso, has also a few other names. Greek and Roman mythology has the name of Bacchus mentioned as the god of wine. Dionysus was another name by which the Greeks had also called him.

Itso did hear it said that Bacchus was not only the god of wine, but also of women and song. To Itso, this is clearly indicative with what is exactly wrong with the behavior of fallen angels.

Above all, Itso does believe that the fallen angels had altered their physical bodies with wine. They therefore had made it impossible for them to please the God of heaven. These very fallen angels were warned by God not to do this to themselves and to other angels around them. When the song of angelic disobedience toward God had been enough, Itso believes that God had then casted out all of the fallen angels in heaven, and then he put them into the universe. (Rev. 12:9).

Fallen angels did not stop their corrupt behavior there in the universe, in Itso's opinion. Upon the earth, the fallen angels had waited for their chance to debase their immoral manner much further. They, the fallen angels, had waited until the corrupted daughters of Adam began to multiply themselves worldwide. Having used their seductive charms upon these disobedient daughters, Itso believes that the fallen angels had succeeded in the production of non-reproductive offspring whose name is known as the Nephilim.

It new becomes interesting and important for Itso to notice two major things about the Nephilim. The first is about the Nephilim in relation to the ancient and worldwide biblical flood that is mentioned in the book of Genesis 6:17. The second major thing would be more detail about Nephilim society and its relationship to the non-believing offspring of Adam.

Great Primeval Flood

Itso had also some major questions which concerns about the ancient, primeval flood that covered the whole earth:

1) What images first come into your mind whenever you consider the possibility of an ancient, primeval flood which covered the entire earth?
2) Did an event such as this in the past actually occur?
3) From the deluge, as described in Genesis 7:17–24, what is such evidence?

In chapter 3, paragraph 9, of the book, *Mankind's Search for God*, Itso had discovered that under the subheading of "The Flood—Fact or Myth?" on page 46 were these things to say about the Nephilim and the flood:

1) "Taking us back to some 4,500 years ago, to about 2,500 BCE, the Bible tells us that rebel spirit sons of God materialized in human form and 'went taking wives for themselves.'"
2) "This unnatural interbreeding produced the violent Nephilim, 'the mighty ones who were of old, the men of fame.'"
3) Their lawless conduct affected the pre-flood world to the point that Jehovah said, "'I am going to wipe men whom I have created off the surface of the ground...because I do regret that I have made them.'"

4) But Noah found favor in the eyes of Jehovah.

5) "The account then continues with the specific and practical steps Noah had to take to save himself, as well as his family and a variety of animal kinds, from the flood (Genesis 6:1–8,13 and 8:22; 1 Peter 3:19,20; 2 Peter 2:4; Jude 6)."

So now Itso does know why God had allowed a worldwide flood to occur upon the face of the earth. It was due to the rebel spirit sons of God (fallen angels) who, as materialized in human form, went to take wives for themselves. These wives, therefore, in Itso's opinion, had to have been from the mortal offspring of Adam, who is God the Father! The violently oppressive Nephilim was therefore produced by this unnatural interbreeding.

The Nephilim, in Itso's view, had appeared at first to have superior intelligence than that of the mortal offspring of God. Itso well does know that appearances can be deceiving, and the Nephilim were quite a deceptive lot! The Nephilim had ultimately became the source for all of the flesh which had corrupted its way upon the earth, as is mentioned in Genesis 6:12. It would not even surprise Itso in the least that the Nephilim were responsible for the creation of the dinosaurs!

In chapter 3, paragraph 10 of *Mankind's Search for God*, Itso had read this about the pre-flood events:

1) "The record of pre-flood events related to Genesis is branded as myth by modern critics."

2) "Yet the history of Noah was accepted and believed by faithful men, such as Isaiah, Ezekiel, Jesus Christ, and the apostles Peter and Paul."

3) "Pre-flood events are also reflected in so many mythologies worldwide."

4) "Mythologies include the ancient Assyro-Babylonian mythology entitled, 'The Epic of Gilgamesh.'"

5) "Other mythologies also include one from China, Aztecs, Incas, and the Maya."

What about "The Flood and the God-Man Gilgamesh" as is the following chapter 3 subheading, in *Mankind's Search for God*? Itso had found that the twelfth paragraph under this subheading on page 48 to be very interesting for it does say:

1) "It is a story of the exploits of Gilgamesh described as being two-thirds god and one-third man, or a demi-god."
2) "Gilgamesh was not exactly a pleasant creature to have around. The inhabitants of Uruk complained to the Gods: 'His lust leaves no virgin to her lover, neither the warrior's daughter nor the wife of the noble.'"

Some questions which Itso now had about Uruk and Gilgamesh, and Lucifer:

1) Was Uruk, most likely a great city, where apparently Gilgamesh had built walls, a great rampart, and a temple there?
2) Was Gilgamesh therefore the first created Nephilim offspring that had ever existed between that of Eve and Lucifer?
3) The very Lucifer who turned into Satan the Devil?

Talk about dysfunctional families as being only just a modern-day phenomenon! thought Itso.

Itso could now see why God, through Adam, had to intervene and to "nip the problem of Gilgamesh in the bud" as it were thereby preventing Satan from using Eve to overthrow God's heavenly authority. Eve eventually came to side with Adam in order to solve the problem of Gilgamesh.

Together, Adam and Eve created what was originally intended to be a human rival of Gilgamesh. This is what Itso most certainly believes as the true sequence of events back then. That true rival to Gilgamesh, therefore, was intended to be the first-born son of Adam and Eve, none other than Cain. It did not turn out, however, to be a rivalry between that of Cain and of Gilgamesh.

In chapter 3, paragraph 13, pages 48–9, with Itso's emphasis in brackets, it says, "What action did the gods [Adam and Christ?] take in response to the people's protest [angelic realm?]? The goddess Arurru [Eve?] created Enkidu [Cain?] to be the human rival of Gilgamesh. However, instead of being enemies, they became close friends. In the course of the epic, Enkidu died. Shattered, Gilgamesh cried: 'When I die, shall I not be like Enkidu? Woe had entered my belly [not able to produce offspring like Cain?] Fearing death, I roam over the steppe.' He wanted the secret of immortality and set out to find Utnapishtim, [Noah?] the deluge survivor who had been given immortality with the gods."

Itso had found quite fascinating that the Utnapishtim in the Epic of Gilgamesh appears to be given the same immortality by the Latter-Day Saint Mormons, which thereby transforms Noah into the angel Gabriel! Itso has more to say about Noah in other world religions also.

Continuing with chapter 3, paragraph 14 on page 49, Itso had found that it says, "Gilgamesh eventually finds Utnapishtim, who tells him the story of the flood. As found in Epic tablet XI, known as the Flood Tablet, Utnapishtim recounts instructions given to him concerning the flood: 'Tear down (this) house, build a ship! Give up possessions, seek thou life…' Aboard the ship take thou the seed of all living things.' Does this sound somewhat similar to the Bible's reference to Noah and the flood? But Utnapishtim cannot bestow immortality upon Gilgamesh. Gilgamesh disappointed, returns home to Uruk. The account concludes with his death. The overall message of the epic is the sadness and frustration of death and the hereafter. Those ancient people did not find the God of truth and hope. However, the epic's link to the Bible's simple account of the pre-flood era is quite evident."

It seems to Itso that the ancient Nephilim were somehow programmed by God to not find the God of truth and hope. That this was somehow God's message to the fallen angel sons of God. The message being that their offspring Nephilim would also be cursed due to their rebellious nature toward the God of Heaven.

From the subtitle of "Flood Legend in Other Cultures," on pages 49–52, Itso had read of other accounts than that of the Assyro-Babylonian Epic of Gilgamesh. An earlier account than that of the Epic of Gilgamesh was that of the Sumerian myth presenting "Zuisudra" as counterpart to the biblical Noah. Itso did find that the name of Zuisudra to be a curious corruption of "Zeus," the Greek ruler of the gods. The Greeks, from Itso's perspective, most likely obtained their god legends from the Sumerian records as did the earlier civilizations of Babylon and Assyria.

Itso had then also read that in the Chinese version of the Deluge, the ancient ruler Yu was the conqueror of the Great Flood. Aztec mythology spoke of the earth inhabited by giants, a reminder of the Nephilim of Genesis 6:4 in the Bible. It also included a Primeval Flood legend and the gods who ruled at that time, with men who were being saved by becoming fish to this day; the fish is symbolic of Christianity.

The Incas of South America, and the Maya in Mexico and in Central America had their flood legend that involved a universal deluge. Itso had this concluded that other flood legends around the world do exist, which also supports the historical event related in the book of Genesis.

At bottom, page 107 of *Mankind's Search for God*, Itso had found a definition of the Hindi "Trimurti." It is listed as the Hindi triad of Brahma, Vishnu, and Siva. Itso believes them to be the basic structure of the Hindu religion which originates in India.

Brahma is listed on page 116 as "the Creator God, the principle of creation in the universe. One of the gods of the 'Trimurti' (triad)."

In absolute Christian terms, Itso believes that Brahma describes none other than Jesus Christ of the Bible. Brahma, to Itso, also appears to be in its origin of spelling the biblical Abraham, who is the patriarch, or father, of many nations (Gen. 17:1–8).

Itso then discovers that Siva, on the other hand, represents all of the dark, destructive spirits and consorts of the Trimurti. Siva is therefore symbolized by the trident and the phallus, as mentioned at the bottom of page 117.

Also listed at bottom of page 117, Itso finds that Vishnu is what the Hindus regard as god, the preserver of life. Vishnu is the third member of the Trimurti.

The point by which Itso is attempting to make here is that within the Trimurti, Brahma represents permanent immortality, or eternal life. Vishnu represents mortality turned to immortality, hence the preserver of life and what Itso believes, is that very Noah of the Bible. Siva, to Itso, thereby represents immortality turned to mortality, or that of fallen angels and in the exact opposite direction from the Kingdom of Heaven!

It is now interesting for Itso to note that Gautama Buddha, founder of the Buddhist religion, is viewed by Hindus as an incarnation, or manifestation (avatar), of Vishnu. There are consorts (wives) and many avatars which do indeed point directly to Vishnu.

There is good reason why Itso would believe that Vishnu is none other than Noah from the Bible book of Genesis. Itso also believes that in accordance with the Latter-Day Mormons book entitled, *History of the Church* by Joseph Smith: "Noah is also the angel Gabriel" (HC 3:386).

For Itso, the Latter-Day-Saint's King James Version of the Holy Bible has this to say about the great primeval flood. It can be found in the left-hand column on page 739 of the *Bible Dictionary*:

1) "The tradition of a great flood is found in nearly every ancient culture.

2) A Babylonian account closely resembles the record in the Bible, but the biblical account differs from all others in its religious value and the purpose of it.

3) The scriptural account teaches that the flood was sent to cleanse the earth because of the wickedness of the people.

4) Noah and his family were saved because they were righteous (Gen.6:9; Moses 8:27).

5) The authenticity of the Genesis account of the flood is confirmed by latter-day revelation as recorded in Moses 7:34, 42–43, 8:8–30, Cf. Ether 13:2."

From *The Routledge Dictionary of Religious and Spiritual Quotations*, Itso has compiled a collection of twelve Primeval Flood notes:

1) God said to Noah, "The end of all flesh is come before me; for the earth is filled with violence through them: and, behold, I will destroy them with the earth. Make thee an ark of gopher wood" (Gen. 6;13–14).

2) "As in the days that were before the flood, they were eating and drinking, marrying and giving in marriage, until the day that Noah entered into the ark" (Matt. 24:38)."

3) It was suggested to Noah, "No more of thy people will believe than have believed already, so be not distressed at what they have been doing. Make the Ark under our eyes" (Koran 11, 38–9).

4) "Tear down this house, build a ship! Give up possessions, seek thou life. Despise property and keep the soul alive! Aboard the ship take thou the seed of all living things." *The Epic of Gilgamesh*, Tablet XI (1200–1000 BCE)

5) The fish said, "In such and such a year that flood will come. Thou shalt then attend to me by preparing a ship: and when the flood has risen thou shalt enter into the ship, and I will save thee from it. The flood then swept away all these creatures, and Manu alone remained here" (Shatapatha Brahmana, i,8,4-6).

6) "You must have an ark built, a sturdy one with a cable tied to it. You will embark on it with seven seers. All the seeds of creatures I have enumerated before, you should place in the ark and then wait for me" (Mahabharata 3, 30).

7) "Zeus in disgust let loose a great flood on the earth, meaning to wipe out the whole race of man; but Deucalion, king of Phthia…built an ark, victualled it, and went aboard with his wife Pyrrha. Robert Graves." *The Greek Myths* (1955)

8) "Athenian: Then what view do you both take of the ancient legends? Have they any truth behind them?
"Clinias: Which legends might you mean?

"Athenian: Those which tell of repeated destructions of mankind by floods, pestilences, and from various other causes, which leave only a handful of survivors…The few who then escaped the general destruction must all have been mountain shepherds, mere scanty embers of humanity." Plato, *Laws* 3, 677

9) "A branch of one of your antediluvian families, fellows that the flood could not wash away." William Congreve, *Love for Love*, volume 2 (1695)
10) "Theirs was the giant race before the flood." John Dryden, *Epistles*, "To Mr. Congreve" (1693)
11) "Apres nous le deluge [after us the flood]. Madame de Pompadour," quoted in Madame de Hausset, *Memoires* (1766)
12) "If I were called in to construct a religion, I should make use of water." Phillip Larkin, *The Whitsun-Weddings* (1964)

By listing all of the Primeval Flood quotations from *The Routledge Dictionary*, Itso's point is to establish the fact that all of the world religions of today seem to have a common beginning, or origin, in that of a primeval flood. What this therefore also says to Itso is that the concept of many nations and languages as Itso does know them today did not come into existence until after the flood as the earth's population began to multiply again.

Itso believes that the same God who brought in the flood and covered the earth with it is therefore the same God, who at the tower of Babel confounded the one language, which up to then, all had spoken together. This confusion of languages, Itso believes, had caused many people from the Babel tower to scatter over all of the earth and into different nations. Itso did find this period of history, mentioned in chapter 11 of the book of Genesis, verses 1–9.

Why would it have been absolutely necessary for God to allow the confusion of the one language, which God's offspring had always spoken, into many, and then scatter all of his people into the many nations that we know of today? Itso had wondered.

Well, Itso believes God saw that by his word, the Nephilim middle-class power was finally broken by the great flood. God was therefore in absolutely no hurry to have his direct offspring imitate the same violent and corrupt behavior their former Nephilim taskmasters had exhibited in pre-flood times!

Nephilim Offspring

As ITSO HAD ALREADY MENTIONED previously, the Nephilim offspring of their fallen-angel fathers were also cursed by mortality and death. They, the Nephilim, may have seemed to be intelligent enough at first glance with their strength, talent, and fame.

However, all of the Nephilim, in Itso's opinion, were unable to multiply any offspring of their own apart from their fallen-angel fathers. The very survival of the Nephilim race depended solely upon the mortal-women rebel-daughters of Adam along with the fallen-angels! (Gen. 6:1–4)

In other words, Itso does believe that all of the Nephilim were automatically born eunuchs! This was their great weakness and their great secret. That the Nephilim were attempting to hide this fact from their non-eunuch subjects should surprise no one. As long as the Nephilim could keep the offspring of God under their subjection and under their own power, they being the Nephilim could continue to keep that secret of theirs hidden.

How did the Nephilim manage to keep their secret hidden from God's offspring? Itso had wondered.

The answer to Itso's question being, that the Nephilim were able to use their vastly superior physical and mental intelligence which they had obtained from their fallen-angel fathers! Going into some detail about the oppressiveness of Nephilim society makes these following Bible verses absolutely believable! Is it any wonder when Genesis 6:5 says "That the wickedness of man was great in the earth, and that every imagination of the thoughts of his heart was only evil continually."

How about what Itso had studied in Genesis 6:6, which says, "And it repented the Lord [Jesus Christ] that he had made man on the earth, and it grieved him at his heart."

So why, therefore, would God's offspring want to submit themselves to the evil, oppressive rule of the Nephilim? Itso had wondered.

For Itso, the answer to the above question being, that not all of Adam's direct offspring did submit themselves to Nephilim rule. In fact, early on in the Nephilim rule, Itso had discovered biblical evidence that some of God's offspring were quite resistant to the Nephilim's oppressive rule over them!

Itso had found that especially resistant to the Nephilim oppressiveness was the offspring resulting from Adam's third child to Eve by the name of Seth. This beautifully explains the exact meaning of Genesis 4:26: "And to Seth, to him also there was born a son; and he called his name Enos: then began men to call upon the name of the Lord [Jesus Christ]."

Itso did discover that generations of Adam unfolding though the lines of Seth and Enos have eventually led us to Enoch, begotten son of Jared. The Enoch of Jared, Itso believes, should therefore not be confused with Enoch, son of Seth's oldest brother Cain. Cain had built the city of Enoch, which he had named after his son, where he lived, in the land of Nod.

Did Cain's half-brother Gilgamesh help in building the city of Enoch? wondered Itso. *The Epic of Gilgamesh may contain a possible answer to this question!* thought Itso.

The Enoch of Jared, on the other hand, is the Enoch who walked closely with God while on earth. This Enoch led the people of God, who also had established God's city of Zion upon the earth, for it stood steadfast against those who had opposed it, chiefly the Nephilim.

Enoch, son of Jared, along with the city of Zion, had later fled into heaven in the many years before the flood as the possible result of nuclear conflict between the war factions in Nephilim society. This, Itso believes, had taken place in the ancient times (Gen. 5:24).

Left behind upon the earth was Methuselah, Enoch's son, who had prophesied about the coming of Noah and the flood. In the time-period between the rapture of Zion into heaven and the flood,

Itso believes that there was a great famine upon the earth. Many had died as a result of this famine. *The Pearl of Great Price* book of Moses mentions about the famine in chapter 8, verse 4.

Was this ancient, worldwide famine the direct result of some ancient nuclear and interplanetary conflict between the warring factions of the Nephilim? Itso had wondered.

Itso did know by now that it was with good reason Adam and Eve had their third child, Seth. This birth had come about after their firstborn child, Cain, had murdered their second-born child whose name was Abel.

Itso had found, according to Genesis 4:2–8, that Abel's work of keeping sheep had pleased the Lord more than Cain's tilling of the ground.

What sin could possibly be laying at Cain's door which would make him jealous of his brother Abel? thought Itso.

In the Latter-Day Saints' book, *The Pearl of Great Price*, in the book of Moses chapter 5, Itso found that verses 26–28 had this to say, "And Cain was wroth [angry] and listened not anymore to the voice of the Lord, neither to Abel, his brother, who walked in holiness before the Lord. And Adam and his wife mourned before the Lord, because of Cain and his brethren. And it came to pass that Cain took one of his brothers' daughters to wife, and they loved Satan more than God."

Obviously, Cain's anger management problem had produced the mess which he got himself into! thought Itso. *Could it be that Satan's first born Nephilim son, Gilgamesh, was also involved in the plot to kill his half-brother Abel?* Itso had wondered.

There is a good reference point that concerns a possible conspiracy between Cain and his half-brother Gilgamesh. That reference point could very well be from "The Epic of Gilgamesh," earlier mentioned by Itso.

What, therefore, do we make of Gilgamesh, who I believe was the first and only Nephilim child created between the serpent (Satan) and Eve? wondered Itso. *A careful examination of Genesis chapter three, verses fourteen, fifteen, and sixteen, in my opinion, speak volumes as to the beginning of the Nephilim offspring!* thought Itso.

"And the Lord God said unto the serpent, Because thou hast done this [produce Nephilim?], thou art cursed above all cattle, and above every beast of the field; upon thy belly shalt thou go, and dust shalt thou eat all the days of thy life:" (v. 14).

So again, what can cattle, and animals on earth do, that the Nephilim race cannot? wondered Itso.

Then the eureka moment had finally occurred to Itso. Itso had finally discovered the answer that he had long been searching for, by the grace of God.

Cattle and animals rapidly reproduce themselves, and multiply like frogs and like rabbits! Itso thought.

"And I will put enmity between thee and the woman, and between thy seed and her seed; it shall bruise thy head, and thou shalt bruise his heel" (v. 15).

A dictionary term that Itso discovered for the word *enmity* is *hatred*. As Itso had well known by now, and has happened, the Nephilim race began to dominate, and then to oppress the non-eunuch offspring of God, most likely to the point of slavery. The head of the Nephilim was bruised, that of the fallen-angels, due to the fact that they had no more spiritual insight toward obedience to none other than the righteousness of God in heaven.

With murderous Cain, firstborn son of Adam and Eve, what Itso does like to call, The Nephilim Gene, was therefore through Eve, automatically transplanted to the non-believing, non-eunuch offspring of God. It was this non-believing, non-eunuch offspring of God which Itso believes had led to the eventual crucifixion of Jesus Christ generations later. Sin indeed comes with its dire consequences! The following, verse 16, makes all of the consequences of sin to be abundantly clear: "Unto the woman he said, I will greatly multiply thy sorrow and thy conception; in sorrow thou shalt bring forth children: and thy desire 'shall be' to thy husband, and he shall rule over thee."

This is why Itso does believe that there were no more Nephilim created between Satan and Eve. That did not stop all the other fallen angels, in the creation of their own Nephilim, who had all originated from the rebellious daughters of Eve!

Itso, in his research, had found very interesting to discern that before there was a flood, a great drought had covered the face of the earth. This meant that many people had died from the ancient drought.

Rivers and lakes evaporating on the earth's surface would most likely have driven the Nephilim from the surface of the earth. Itso believes that they, the Nephilim, would mostly have gone to underground sources of water, and where subterranean cities would be built by them.

That our non-eunuch offspring of God would have, at one time in the ancient past, before the flood, been living in caves does not at all surprise Itso. The heat and humidity from the sun and from any lingering nuclear fallout in those days had become so unbearable on the earth's surface that the caves would have been the believing non-eunuch offspring's only protection from the drought and the famine.

The technical and economic superiority of the Nephilim in those days would have meant that the unbelieving non-eunuch offspring of God had depended on the Nephilim for their very survival. Survival, therefore, had meant the food and water of which the Nephilim had control.

Itso believes that the Nephilim also had control of all earth's animal kingdom to the point whereby they could, from their underground cities, genetically engineer certain beasts without God's permission. These kind of animals are generally classified as dinosaurs by Itso's modern terminology of them. This would yet, in Itso's opinion, explain Genesis 6:12 in the Bible, which says, "And God looked upon the earth, and, behold, it was corrupt: for all flesh had corrupted his way upon the earth."

In Itso's opinion, the Nephilim must have accounted for the possibility of a future flood, which would have quickly erased their underground cities, making them uninhabitable. There was a possibility of another planet, Mars, with an atmosphere about similar to what earth's was before the drought. This fact alone would have caused some of the Nephilim to move from earth to Mars, even before the deluge, was apparent upon the earth. Itso does believe that the space vehicles, which they, the Nephilim, must have copied from their fallen-angel fathers would surely have been sufficient enough to have taken the Nephilim to Mars!

Alas, with the passage of the flood on our earth, and with some time passed, Itso believes that some of the Nephilim had managed to return to earth again with some of their ships. To their utter disappointment, the few Nephilim that did return had come to the realization that things on earth could never be the same way as when they had left the earth before to escape both the drought and the flood.

With their numbers greatly reduced as well as their technical, economical, and intellectual capacity diminished as a result of the flood, Itso believes that the Nephilim must have known that theirs was a culture that was quickly dying out. Space travel had greatly altered the shape of their fallen-angel fathers to the point where the fallen angels were no longer able to produce any Nephilim at all. A thinning atmosphere on the surface of planet Mars did mean that life for the Nephilim there on Mars was not in any way better than it was on earth before the flood.

Itso believes that the Nephilim faced the same issues of mortality in their underground colonies on Mars, much like they did in their below-ground cities on planet earth. It would not have mattered to Itso, or anyone, whether the maximum lifespan of a Nephilim was roughly seven-hundred years old in comparison with the maximum lifespan of the non-Nephilim offspring of God which was now reduced to 120 years due to the drought. The result of death for both Nephilim and non-Nephilim was exactly the same, and they both knew about it then!

Yes, Itso does believe, that the few Nephilim who had managed to return to earth again after the flood must have thus known that their own numbers and lifespan indeed had limits to them. The few remaining Nephilim must have realized that if you cannot beat the offspring of God on this planet of earth, then you might as well join them.

It does not, therefore, take a giant leap of imagination for Itso to figure out that while some of those priestly Nephilim were still alive and kicking, they would think to leave the non-Nephilim offspring of God a record of their past existence. In the event that the Nephilim do indeed completely die out of existence is with good reason that the remaining Nephilim would surely leave a record of their own existence in the midst of non-Nephilim!

All of these certain possibilities have allowed Itso to ask some further questions about what really has been going on in earth's history:

1) Would there be in existence a library of records anywhere in heaven or on earth where the records of the Nephilim are kept?

2) What possible event, could have brought about a sudden worldwide drought over the entire earth around and about the same time that the city of Zion, or the New Jerusalem, had fled into heaven?

3) Did atomic warfare suddenly erupt between the warring factions of the ancient Nephilim?

4) Did some of the Nephilim escape to the planet of Mars as a result?

5) Was there also some sort of "Interplanetary Warfare" between the earth and Mars, which had resulted in the creation of the moon?

6) How about the possibility that the genetic mutations from atomic warfare also produced, or led, to the production of the dinosaurs?

7) Was the green Jade material, commonly found in India and China, also the result of ancient atomic warfare?

Atomic warfare in the past and atomic warfare now, what all of this can only tell Itso is that there really is not anything new under the sun. Nothing new under the sun is therefore a true confirmation with the book of Ecclesiastes 1:9–11. Itso thus does believe that history is capable of repetition, although it is never in exactly the same way.

Itso had revealed about an ancient nuclear war which had suddenly erupted as the city of Zion, the New Jerusalem, had fled directly into heaven. Another nuclear war on earth was also due to erupt when the city of New Jerusalem had appeared once again in the sky of Heaven for all who are on the earth to see!

Jesus Christ had truly given the Jonah sign that his church was built upon the earth in three days. Itso believes that this sign is as certain and as sure as Jonah the prophet who was in the belly of the whale for a total of three days and three nights (Jonah 1:17)!

The three-day Feast of Pentecost is what Itso believes that Jesus Christ has been in reference to as a part of his plan of salvation. This is a feast that begins with the first trumpet blast, signifying the rapture of the true church of Philadelphia. It is also a feast which ends three days later with a second and final blast of the trumpet as the rest of the true church of Philadelphia is thus resurrected. See 1 Corinthians 15:51–54 and 1 Thessalonians 4:13–18.

At the sounding of the last trump of Pentecost does this therefore open the door for the Feast of Trumpets to begin. Itso believes that this is when a major earthquake disaster and a sudden outbreak of World War III begin.

The Feast of Atonement is actually what takes place in the aftermath of World War III. This is in actual reality the 'great tribulation period,' during which the 'third Jewish temple' is constructed. It is also a period of time that immediately comes before the Millennium of Jesus Christ's kingdom in Itso's own estimation.

When the one-thousand-year millennium had come to an end, the third Jewish temple (Rev. 21:22) will be no more. It is then that the city of New Jerusalem (Zion) comes down from God (Rev. 21:2,10), out of heaven, prepared as a bride adorned for her husband. God then mentions in Revelation 21:4 that there shall be no more tears, death, sorrow, crying, nor any pain as these have now passed.

Chapter Six

The Final Destination

Spirit River Retreat

As Itso was exiting his window seat on the bus, he does remember going past the aisle seat beside him where Michael was sitting. To this day, Itso did not recall if there was any of Michael's physical presence as Itso had attempted to quickly squeeze by Michael and into the aisle.

Itso then moved to the same front-row aisle seat near to the bus driver where Michael did previously sit earlier. Itso was now momentarily waiting to exit the bus when it had come to its full stop at the Grande Prairie station.

Who exactly was the true identity of this mesomorphically built bus driver talking cordially to the mesomorphic Michael outside of the bus when the vehicle was back at the Valley View bus depot in Alberta? thought Itso. *Could He, the bus driver, have been Jesus Christ in uniform?* Itso had wondered.

Itso could not help but to overhear him speak in glowing terms to the surrounding bus passengers all about his heavenly family. Family is the big thing in the Kingdom of Heaven. It is what Itso knew. Those Christ-like eyes of his and pleasant voice had seemed, therefore, to pierce entirely through Itso's very own soul!

Shortly before Itso had finally exited the bus, Itso had suddenly looked behind him to see if Michael was still sitting in the same aisle seat that he had passed moments ago. What Itso had then noticed was that Michael was still there in the same aisle seat as before. Before, that is, until Itso had then noticed that Michael had quickly arisen from his own aisle seat and had moved to take the window seat that Itso had vacated only moments earlier. To have witnessed this scene with his own eyes, Itso could not help but to have felt that he was strangely and also wonderfully comforted.

He really was watching over me at Grande Prairie just as he said that he would, Itso thought. *How can you not put your own trust in a being such as this!*

After the normal introductory greetings were exchanged with the young elders from the retreat, Itso's large brown leather suitcase was already in the back of the pickup truck. At a local Grande Prairie motel, Itso and company had stayed in separate rooms for the rest of the entire night.

When early the next morning came, and the sun had now completely arisen above the horizon, Itso had found himself riding in the middle of the truck cab, between the male driver and his female sister, on the cab's passenger side. Itso then commenced upon the last part of his trip to the Spirit River retreat. Itso had reached the retreat after roughly about an hour of driving through such roadside communities as Clairmont, Sexsmith, Webster, Woking, Rycroft, and finally, to Spirit River.

Itso and the young elders had now turned off from the main road and onto the long, flat, unpaved laneway which led directly to the main retreat building. The retreat house appeared modern, and it was not much larger than an average home in size.

Itso had stayed with his suitcase in an unfinished wing addition of the retreat house that was under construction. Dry-walled and unpainted, the unfurnished room had only consisted of a bare wooden floor. It had a large opening for where the window was to go on the opposite wall, which faced directly across from the doorway entrance to the room.

Understandably, Itso did become very chilly there on the floor at night inside of the zippered sleeping bag that he had unpacked from out of his suitcase. Itso became uncertain as to how much longer he would have to be sleeping on the bare floor at night. The only source of heating that was given to Itso under those rather clammy conditions was with a kerosene lamp.

A few days later, Itso was put into a separate, portable type mini-trailer with some proper heating and furniture. The portable mini-trailer was only a short distance away from the retreat house's vegetable garden, which was about made to be ready for spring planting.

Mealtimes at the retreat house were in a proper-sized finished and furnished dining area. The quality and quantity of food was at an adequate level. Any possible food fights, which were most possibly happening behind Itso's back, he need not to make mention of.

Itso had remembered that the spiritual retreat's matriarch had tried to impress her unruly family upon him at the dinner table. She did shout the word *example* over and over again. Itso was, to say the least, not too impressed by that episode. Her apparently unaccomplished dream to one day become a dietician as a result of other plans that got in the way, had not really helped Itso's situation.

How do you even begin to tell these people at the dinner table that I, Itso, was actually having an intelligent conversation with the Archangel Michael while on the bus! thought Itso.

After church on Sunday, Itso was allowed to play a game of baseball with the community. Which team had won, Itso did not remember, but the game was enjoyable.

To the pickup truck, with Itso who now sat on back of its loading bed, as it was about ready to leave the community ballfield. That was when Itso had witnessed a guy from one of the ball teams who had approached, climbed the truck's load bed, and had sat near Itso.

Itso had assumed by then that the guy who now sat near Itso must have been a local friend of the family that owned the spiritual retreat. He had needed a ride back to his home, which was along the way back to the retreat now that the baseball game was finished and complete.

Itso had estimated him to be in the mid- to late teens. He had beady looking eyes, was average in height, but maybe was a bit shorter than Itso. He had long blond curly hair flapping over his ears, above his shoulders. He also wore red, black, and white running shoes.

He once asked Itso whether Itso had wanted to go skinny-dipping with him in a nearby pond. For obvious reasons, Itso's spiritual needs were more important to Itso than any fleshly desires at that time. So Itso had instantly and wisely made the right decision and had declined his offer.

Whether that baseball-team guy had gone to the pond and had skinny-dipped by himself, or with someone else, is anyone's guess, that of Itso included. All of which Itso had known back then was that Itso was in absolutely no mood for creating a scandal of any kind at the spiritual retreat or for tarnishing his rather fragile reputation as a stranger there any further.

In the midst of the following weeks, Itso was outside in the garden adjacent to the retreat house, digging up old potatoes and planting rows of new ones to start the season. Itso had at least thought that they were potatoes from what he had been told to plant.

Itso had momentarily glanced over to the other garden plot that was next to his. Itso had noticed that the retreat's matriarch was also hard at work in planting something else, possibly some flowers in Itso's estimation from what he did observe on that day. Someone was definitely watching over Itso to be sure.

Now it was easy to say that Itso had quickly become rather bored with this line of work, planting potatoes. After all, to Itso, there really were no wage incentives whatsoever here. This experience had caused Itso to guess, rightly or wrongly at the time, on the entire point of actually doing any volunteer work at all.

There really was no monetary remuneration at the end of a hard day's work of planting potatoes! thought Itso.

The results of Itso's stay at the Spirit River retreat, located north of Grande Prairie, Alberta, Canada? It was a few predictable weeks that had indeed passed by. Anything else worthy of Itso's remembrance during that time was a steady reminder by strangers and people of the area that Itso was actually lying in "God's country."

As if Itso did not already know who God was that what an irony, really, was Itso's meeting with Michael along the way to Spirit River and on a bus that had travelled from Whitecourt to Grande Prairie! Evidently then, Itso was needing no further prompting that this was God's country. Nevertheless, that prompting is exactly what Itso had gotten!

It was now a few weeks later, at the beginning of June 1984. Itso returned to Central Ontario as he had used the same bus route as the one that he had taken previously to go to Alberta. Itso's humble life had resumed now once more in Ontario.

From this point on, Itso's life was never to be the same again regardless of whether or not Itso had even realized that it was a fact. Itso would never ever forget his second vision or encounter of Michael, which Itso had experienced earlier on the bus in Alberta. No, Itso's life was never to be the same upon his return to Ontario from Alberta.

How little had been known of the interview that Itso had with Michael on the bus. How little had been known that Itso's entire life had changed so profoundly that day, and much more as the years passed by.

A great test of faith and patience was at the utmost for Itso at that time. This was because so little was known then. Itso could not tell them about his second vision-encounter. Itso's second vision-encounter with none other than God the Father himself.

Light Meets Library Café

TWENTY YEARS HAD NOW PASSED since Itso had returned to Ontario from Alberta. To this day, Itso still had all of the bus-ticket stubs in his possession, dated from then. Itso's large brown leather suitcase that he had taken with him on the bus trip remained under his bed. The sleeping bag had, by now, long disappeared from view.

The end-time rapture book that Itso had then was still in his possession as he would await for the next meeting with God at a future time. As it had happened, the wait was not too long, and Itso had needed no suitcase this time.

November of 2001 was when Itso did begin to do some volunteer work at the local Temple Public Library Café stand. Displays there of coffee urns, candy, chocolate bars, cookies, soup, tea, and hot chocolate bags had reminded Itso somewhat of the food that he had back in the Winnipeg bus-terminal cafeteria.

With a little bit of time and some practice, Itso had gradually became proficient in the ringing of cash-register sales. Most customers do appreciate the library café as a place for some quick food and drink especially around the middle of the day, at lunchtime.

Itso had met different types of customers there at the café. Some rich, some poor, some their children, and some without. Some customers simply liked to chat about everything under the sun, while others basically did not like to talk nearly as much, or even at all.

Then came that miraculously wonderful kind of a day in late June of 2004. Itso had found the weather to be both hot and humid all that day. Itso had recalled that it must have been during the early part of the afternoon, long before it was sunset.

Itso had taken notice of a strangely familiar looking man who seemed to be talking amidst a small group of people who were standing a short distance away. Itso could not help but to observe how sharply well-dressed he was in appearance. Not in white robe nor in blue windbreaker jacket. No, Itso could now see that he was in more colorful clothes now in comparison to what he had worn before.

Itso had continued to glance in his direction as he had slowly walked up to the café counter. He then did proceed to order his coffee. When he finished his coffee, he then said something to Itso that made him completely stunned and speechless. He said something like: "Don't forget to refill the urns. They're empty, son."

Itso had then proceeded to pull one of the coffee urns from off its mounted base, and sure enough, the coffee urn was completely empty. When Itso went to check upon the other two urns, Itso had also found that they too were totally in an empty state. All three of the urns were therefore in complete emptiness, just as he had said that they were.

How odd was this? Itso thought. *I always remembered to keep those coffee urns full!*

Itso had now taken one of the urns to the coffee-making machine located on the back countertop beside the sink. Itso then proceeded to fill-up the urn with coffee until it was completely full. With the full urn, Itso then went back to the front countertop. On top of its normal resting stand, Itso was about to replace the urn.

When Itso had looked past the counter to see if Michael was still standing there, Itso had then proceeded to witness quite a spectacular phenomenon! Michael had seemed to be disappearing into a bright, yellowish cloud of light! Itso could not grasp fully any meaning or significance of the sight for which he did see nearby, even as this certain vision was actually happening.

Itso's eyes had continued to be transfixed upon the vision of light which had taken place out front in the existing floor space. That floorspace is the space which lies between the front café counter and spans directly across to the two bottled soft drink machines.

These are the two machines which Itso could see standing out on the floor and along one side of a brick wall. They face almost directly across from the front café counter stand at the opposite end of the floor space. Itso had become both very truly amazed and apprehensive over what had happened next!

Intersecting Worlds

AT THE EXACT SAME TIME as the vanishing cloud, Itso could also now see that a female employee of the library staff was walking past the front café counter. She was on her way toward the double doors of a meeting room. On the outer side of the meeting room was a brick wall spanned between the front café counter stand on the right side of the double doors. Also, the two cold-drink machines by the doors, left side.

Itso had observed, as she walked nonstop and through Itso's vision of Michael's disappearance, by which Itso had currently experienced at the exact same time! Itso also had noticed that her facial expression did not indicate in any way that she did witness anything unusual! Itso had thus believed that he was simultaneously in experience of an intersection between the two worlds—that of the mortal versus that of the world of immortality.

This has got to be the greatest gift of the Holy Spirit which can be bestowed upon any mortal human being! thought Itso.

The yellow cloud was a clear enough indication to Itso that not everyone at the library had witnessed the same phenomenon that Itso had seen. In fact, it had seemed to Itso that he might have been the only one there who had witnessed the vision of God at the library café. A witness, which did include his other angels.

That Michael would be in conversation with a small group of his holy angels nearby would not come as a complete surprise at all to Itso. God does send them across Itso's path every now and then to watch over and to encourage Itso. As it was before, Itso had found that Michael had not a set of wings to flap around in, and neither did the angelic host. Their appearance was like Itso's, only more so.

Also was the reassurance that Michael did call Itso "son," in reference to the coffee urns to be filled. Itso had believed Michael did say that he was watching over Itso in Grande Prairie during Itso's second vision-encounter of him. This was Itso's interpretation. Itso could only guess that the vision encounter back then would as well meant the vision of him at the Temple Public Library Café.

Itso does well recall that Michael's "'Got to go to sleep now,' repeated once" statement has a total of twenty consonants. Also, that Michael's "pitted sunflower seeds" does have a total of twenty letters.

Have twenty consonants and twenty letters anything to do with the twenty years elapsed between my second and third visionary encounters with Michael? Itso thought.

What Itso had referred to here was the period which was between 1984 to 2004. Now Itso had guessed that this was something to think about when it is in reference to the Second Advent of Christ.

Itso did again remember his parent's house back in Angus, Ontario, Canada, when they had ownership of it in the 1960s and early 1970s. That very house was where Itso had his first visions of the Archangel Michael who was dressed in a white robe.

Itso's parents did sell that house in Angus back in the year 1975. The sale had occurred within a few years after they had previously moved away to another new home which was in a rural locality.

Shortly after Itso's mother's passing away in the autumn of 2014, Itso had the rural estate sold by the spring of 2015. As far as Itso was able to tell, the house in Angus, as well as the rural estate were both still in existence up to now.

There is a certain possibility that the white-robed visionary encounters that Itso had of the Archangel Michael back in the late spring of 1967 were meant for the purpose of timed prophecy. By timed prophecy, Itso does have a belief for it to mean exactly forty-five day-years which does exist between the 1,290 days of Daniel 12:11 and Daniel 12:12. Itso had earlier remembered reading that chapter 12, verse 12 of the book of Daniel mentions 1,335 days!

Why else, would God not have spoken at all, during the entire time of my white-robed visionary encounters of Him? Itso wondered.

Why else? It is because Michael had needed not to say anything at all to Itso at that time, during the Arab-Israeli six-day war. The sheer spectacle of Michael's presence, as well as the timing of his presence, had spoken volumes already as to its purpose and its meaning!

Some will certainly argue that there is no connection at all between the white-robed vision encounters of Michael which Itso did have back in June of 1967 and the Armageddon battle of 2024. What Itso will now say about this line of thinking is to just let the facts speak for themselves. Itso believes that the facts do most certainly speak for themselves.

What, then, of a nuclear war in 2020 followed by the battle of Armageddon in 2024? Itso wondered.

Anything thus more specific for Itso to say about the subject of nuclear war in public at the library café could not be known. Itso could not tell. Itso could not tell them of his third visionary-encounter with God.

Was it Michael's hand that wrote those four words on the ancient Babylonian palace wall in plain sight of King Belshazzar? wondered Itso.

Itso does certainly believe that it was indeed Michael's own hand whose four words had signaled the imminent downfall of King Belshazzar's reign. Whose very same words continue to thunder down through the ages to our very day today. Whose hand does rock the cradle of our civilization.

Back in "The Journey", Chapter One, Itso had mentioned, that "The Ancient of Days" could only therefore refer to the "Adam" of Genesis, and the "Archangel Michael" of Revelation, as one and the same person, and not two separate people! If it were so, that "Adam" and the "Archangel Michael", were entirely separate beings, then why is it that God, through Jesus Christ the creator, would indeed "bring the entire animal kingdom to Adam, just to see what He would name them", as is stated in the book of Genesis? (Gen. 2:19)

All this in itself will lead Itso to therefore believe that Jesus Christ is the creator of all things. Jesus has therefore in charge the person of "Ancient of Days, Jehovah, Archangel Michael, Adam", over the "intersecting worlds", of "the Angelic Relm, the Animal Kingdom, and the Mortal, Human Kingdom!"

From Itso's viewpoint, Jesus Christ really is "King of Kings" and "Lord of Lords", "first born from the dead of the Angelic Relm", and from the "Omnipotent and Omnipresent Holy Spirit of Jehovah". This therefore, describes the true "Trinity" and the true "Family of God", as is opposed to the "three persons in one trinity", counterfeit of Satan the Devil! (Rev. 16:13-14)

Itso did know one thing. It was that when you do happen to put your own faith and trust in God, then he will not leave nor forsake you. Being as God is, he was the ultimate old of friends from Angus, whom Itso did not meet while he was in Winnipeg, but on a bus in Alberta. This is now Itso's advice to any weary traveler who is out there:

> "Pay attention to the stranger that you happen
> to meet on your next bus trip. He really could
> be God!"

Itso's express conclusion is that the church rapture of 1,290 days shall begin at precisely the time when Germany turns completely to radical Islam. This event also signifies the Feast of the Unleavened Bread to that of the Pentecost Feast. All feast events are in Jesus Christ's plan of salvation!

The 1,290-day rapture of God's true church is greater than the simultaneous rule of antichrist. Death of antichrist rule really is swallowed up in the victory that is the rapture of the true church!

After 1,290 days is the Feast of Trumpets, which is 45 days in length. After the trumpets, is the Feast of Atonement. Itso believes that the third Jewish temple will be built, and built during this 1,260-day period.

Yes, this is Itso's story. This is Itso's own storybook. The very storybook of which Itso was most surely commissioned by Michael himself to write. The blessings of Michael to that of Itso's soul were meant to be certain!

May God in heaven especially be a blessing to those who do read Itso's story to the point that it is well understood. Itso did finally say to all who are so very faithful in the fellowship of Jesus Christ, the Son of God, amen.

Notes

Chapter 1: The Journey

i)   White Robe
     a) *The New Testament of Our Lord and Saviour Jesus Christ with Psalms and Proverbs*, Authorized King James version (Philadelphia, PA: The Gideons International In Canada, 1968).
     b) "Raindrops Keep Falling on My Head" by Ian Thomas
     c) "Put Your Hand in the Hand" by Anne Murry
     d) "Four Strong Winds" by Ian Tyson

ii) Questions on the Bus
     a) Sir Winston Churchill (1874–1965)
     b) Lindsey, Hal, *The Rapture: Truth or Consequences* (Bantam Book, 1983).

iii) Winnipeg Terminal
     a) Winnipeg Bus Terminal—cafeteria
     b) Temple Public Library Café.

iv) Stops In-Between
     a) Lindsey, Hal, *The Rapture: Truth or Consequences* (Bantam Book, 1983).

v) Another Angel?
   a) Lindsey, Hal, *The Rapture: Truth or Consequences* (Bantam Book, 1983).
   b) "Three Angels' Messages," *Holy Bible: Old and New Testaments in the Authorized King James Version* (C. D. Stampley Enterprises, Inc., 1985) Rev.14:6–13

vi) Windbreaker Blue
   a) About Adam and Eve?
   b) Mormon Church of Jesus Christ of Latter-day Saints, Salt Lake City, Utah, USA
   c) Temple Public Library Café.

vii) "Don't Give Me That"
   a) Lindsey, Hal, *The Rapture: Truth or Consequences* (Bantam Book, 1983).

viii) Watching over Me
   a) Spirit River retreat, northern Alberta, Canada, 1984.

ix) The Witness Book
   a) New World Translation of the Holy Scriptures, New World Bible Translation Committee, Revised 1984 (Watchtower Bible and Tract Society of New York, Inc.).

x) A Test of Numbers
   a) From a newspaper article about the nine-eleven terrorist attacks
   b) *Authorized King James Version* (1985) Rev. 12:4; Exodus 20:1–11

xi) "Got to Go to Sleep Now"
   a) Lindsey, Hal, *The Rapture: Truth or Consequences* (Bantam Book, 1983).
   b) The Barrie Examiner—newspaper

c) Maxwell, Mervyn Ph.D., "The Message of Daniel for You and Your Family," *God Cares, Volume One* (Pacific Press Publishing Association, 1981)
d) Maxwell, Mervyn, Ph.D., "The Message of Revelation for You and Your Family," *God Cares, Volume Two* (Pacific Press Publishing Association, 1985)
e) Letters c) and d) above refer to materials used to complete the Bible prophecy courses.

Chapter 2: The Church

i) Five Loaves and Two Witnesses
  a) Maxwell, *God Cares, Volume One.*
  b) Maxwell, *God Cares, Volume Two*
  c) *Authorized King James Version*
    -Rev. 2,3:7–8,14:6–13
    -1 Thess. 4:13–18
    -1 Cor.15:51–58
    -John 3:16
    -Matt. 25:1–13

ii) Diasporas One and Two
  a) *Authorized King James Version*, Dan 9:2
  b) *Book of Mormon*, 3 Nephi 8:5–7
  c) *Pay Attention to Daniel's Prophecy* (Brooklyn, NY: Watchtower Bible and Tract Society of New York, Inc., 1999) ch.14, pp. 240.

iii) Diaspora Three
  a) *Authorized King James Version*
    -Rev. 2, 3:7–13,14:6–13
    -Ezek. 1:16

iv) World Trade Center
  a) World Trade Center Bombing, February 1993.

b) Prophetic Conference, Saturday, May 2, 1998 at Barrie District Central Collegiate

c) September 11, 2001.

v) Repeating Numbers
   a) Consonants and Vowels.
   b) Seventeen letters equals seventeen years.
   c) Thirty-four letters equals thirty-four years.
   d) Number thirty-four reduced to seven.
   e) Number seven indicates completeness of God's creation and the millennium.
   f) Twenty consonants equals twenty years.
   g) Alphabet-consonant *e* plus alphabet-consonant *o* totals twenty years while vowel *e* times two, plus vowel *o* times five, repeated once, equals fourteen years, for a total sum of thirty-four years.

vi) Emerging Patterns
   a) Twenty-five vowels equals seven (two plus five).
   b) Handwriting on the wall.
   c) 1984 plus 25 years of vowels equals 2009.

vii) The Right Direction?
   a) Righteous going in opposite direction to Wicked.
   b) Armstrong, Herbert W., "The Separation of the Birthright. and the Sceptre," *The United States and Britain in Prophecy* (Worldwide Church of God, October 1984) ch.4, pp. 29–46.
   c) *Authorized King James Version*
      -Isa. 14:12–15;
      -Rev. 6:1–8

   d) Orwell, George, *1984* (Penguin Books, 1954).
   e) *New World Translation of the Holy Scriptures* (Brooklyn, NY: Watchtower Bible and Tract Society of New York, Inc., 1984; 1961, 1981, 1984).

viii) Three Millennium Concepts
  a) Lindsey, Hal, The Rapture: Truth or Consequences (Bantam Book, 1983) p.27, 29.
  b) Ibid., p.30. "Roots of Anti-Semitism."
  c) Ibid., p.b.166. "The Prophetic Books Unsealed," ch.12.
  d) Ibid., b.p.166–t.p.167. "A Short History of Prophetic Interpretation."
  e) Ibid., p.167. "Prophecy's Dark Ages," Augustine.
  f) Ibid., p.167. "Augustine's Influence."
  g) Ibid., p.168–9. "The Period of Prophetic Ferment."
  h) *Authorized King James Version*
     -Rev. 2:18–24, Thyatira church.
     -Rev. 6:1–8, Four Horsemen.

Chapter 3: The Four Horsemen

  i) Horseman One
    a) *Authorized King James Version*
       -Rev. 2:6,14,15
       -Rev. 6:2
       -Dan. 2:45; Jesus Christ, "The Stone,"

    b) *The Encyclopedia Americana International Edition* (2002)
       -"Constantine I, Roman Emperor," 7; 647–649;
       -"Council of Nicaea," 20:301.

    c) Ibid., "Constantine and Christianity."
    d) *Nostradamus For Dummies**, c.2005
    e) *These Times: The Amazing Prophecies of Daniel and Revelation* (Hagerstown, MD: Review and Herald Publishing Association, 1983)
    f) *The World Book Encyclopedia* (Chicago, IL: World Book, Inc., 2006)

-"Constantine I," CI:993;
-"Nicene Councils," N:402.

g) Findley, Mark A., *The Almost Forgotten Day* (Siloam Springs, AR: Concerned Group, Inc., 1988) pp.57, 60.

h) Marcussen, Jan A., *National Sunday Law* (Thompsonville, IL: Amazing Truth Publications, 1983).
-Appendix 12, "Time Not Lost."

i) Ibid. ch.3, p.23, "The Beast Described."

j) Reference to Augustine's book, *City of God*, from previous chapter.

ii) Horseman Two
a) Authorized King James Version, Rev. 6:4
b) "Napoleon Bonaparte," *The Encyclopedia Americana International Edition* (Danbury, CT: Grolier Educational, 2002) pp. 19:728–33.
c) Ibid., "Peace and Reform"
d) Ibid., "Man and Legend."
e) "Napoleon I," *The World Book Encyclopedia* (Chicago, IL: World Book, Inc., 2006) NI: 6–9.
f) Ibid., vol. N, p.19 "The Empire of Napoleon I."
g) Wigal, Donald Ph.D., *Visions of Nostradamus and Other Prophets* (Owings Mills, MD: Ottenheimer Publishers Inc., 1998) b.p.31
h) Kane, Perry, "The Modern Age and the First Antichrist," *Nostradamus and the Millennium: What May Be Coming* (1999) b.p.19–t.p.20,
i) Ovason, David, *Nostradamus—Prophecies for America* (New York, NY: Avon Books, 2001) pp.14, 63–9.

iii) Horseman Three
a) *Authorized King James Version*
-Rev. 6:5–6

b) "Hitler," *The World Book Encyclopedia* (Chicago, IL: World Book, Inc., 2006) H: 264–7.

c) Ibid., vol. N:550; "Nostradamus."

d) "Hitler," *The Encyclopedia Americana International Edition* (Danbury, CT: Grolier Educational, 2002) pp. 14:246–9.

e) Ibid., p.248; "Dictatorship: 1933–1945."

f) Ibid., p.248; "Consolidation of Power."

g) Smolley, Richard, "Century II, Quatrain 24," *The Essential Nostradamus* (New York, NY: Penguin Group (USA.) Inc., 2006) b.p.84–t.p.85.

h) Wigal, Donald Ph.D., *Visions of Nostradamus and Other Prophets* (Owings Mills, MD: Ottenheimer Publishers Inc., 1998) b.p.31–t.p.32.

iv) Horseman Four

a) *Authorized King James Version*
   -Rev. 6:8
   -Ezek. 38:2
   -Ezek. 39:6

b) Roberts, Henry, *The Complete Prophecies of Nostradamus* (Three Rivers Press, 1999) pp.63, 187, 292

c) Ibid., p.63; "'Century Two, quatrain sixty-two."

d) Ibid., p.187; "'Century Six, quatrain twenty-four."

e) Ibid., p.292; "'Century Nine, quatrain forty-four."

f) Wigal, Donald Ph.D., *Visions of Nostradamus and Other Prophets* (Owings Mills, MD: Ottenheimer Publishers Inc., 1998) p.34.

Chapter 4: The Statues of Great Tribulation

i) September Eleven

a) Ovason, David, *Nostradamus—Prophecies for America* (New York, NY: Avon Books, 2001) pp.14.

ii) Earthquakes, Radiation, and Disease
    a) Chamberlain, E. R., "II Diagnosis," *Jackdaw Fifty* (1973)
    b) Chamberlain, E. R., "The Black Death," *Jackdaw Fifty* (1973)
    c) Astronomers:
        i) Copernicus (1473–1543)
        ii) Galileo (1564–1642)

iii) Itso's Christ Vision
    a) Death of Itso's father six months later.
    b) COKE, an acronym which means, "Christ of Kingdom Eternal"?

iv) Sabbath Day Remembrance
    a) "Keep the Sabbath day to sanctify it, as the Lord thy God hath commanded thee"
        -Deut. 5:12

v) Meaning of Seven Annual Festivals
    a) God's master plan of Salvation
    b) Seven Annual Festivals include:
        i) Passover,
        ii) Days of Unleavened Bread,
        iii) Pentecost,
        iv) Feast of Trumpets,
        v) Day of Atonement,
        vi) Feast of Tabernacles, and
        vii) The Last Great Day

vi) Bridging the Church Wheels of Time
    a) Wheels of time moving through all seven festivals of God's salvation plan.
    b) Bridge of time, formed by three of the festivals that is:
        i) Pentecost,
        ii) Trumpets, and
        iii) Atonement.

c)   Sun, Moon, and Stars (symbols)
     -Rev. 12:1;17;14

vii) Nebuchadnezzar's Image versus the Handwriting on the Wall
   a)   The four handwriting words of Daniel 5:25–28 had dovetailed beautifully with Nebuchadnezzar's image of Daniel 2:31–45.
   b)   Clay divisions: miry clay versus potter's clay.

viii) A Soldier Statue of Iron
   a)   Iron Soldier statue vision that was revealed by God between 2011 to 2014.
   b)   Iron Statue standing at narrow end of rectangular pool.
   c)   Statue broken, swallowed by water in pool.

ix) Iron Soldier versus Nebuchadnezzar's Image
   a)   Iron Soldier to come to power; shortly before the great tribulation begins.
   b)   Unholy alliance between the shattered iron of Daniel 2:40 and that of the moist, miry clay.
   c)   Unholy alliance is in total contrast to, and totally divided from, the molded potter's clay.

x)   Two Generational Cycles Times Five
   a)   Economic cycles of fifteen years.
   b)   Political cycles of nineteen years.

xi) Convergence and Divergence Points of Cycles Fifteen and Nineteen
   a)   Year 2005, the year both cycles of fifteen and nineteen had converged in that same year.
   b)   Years 2020–2024, is greatest divergence of the two cycles, allowing enough time for the great tribulation to occur.

xii) Other Generational Cycles
   a)   Spiritual cycles of seventy-years length.
   b)   Judgment cycles of forty-years length.

xiii) Last Judgment Cycle and Great Tribulation
   a)   Great Tribulation occupies the final four years of the judgement cycle concurrently, between the years of 2020 and 2024.
   b)   *Mystery of the Ages* (USA: Philadelphia Church of God, 1985, 2009) Second Edition, p. 122.

xiv) Temple Code Solved
   a)   Literal and allegorical methods involved to solve the Temple "Code"
   b)   Starting and ending points provided
   c)   Supernatural code, by existence and origin
   d)   Compatible and comparable to the Bible code
   e)   Able to explain its own prophetic symbolism complementary to the Bible

xv) The Reign of Antichrist
   a)   Middle of antichrist reign of seven years, interrupted by a major nuclear war.
        - Daniel 12;11–12

   b)   Lesser Tribulation period (1,290 days) abruptly ends (earthquake) forty-five days before the greater tribulation (1,260 days) begins

xvi) Summer and Winter Solstices
   a)   *Authorized King James Version*
        -Matt. 24:32–33
        -Matt. 24:20–21
        -Rev. 13:4–5

   b)   Chr.ch 17:10–14
        -Third Temple prophecy

Chapter 5: The Great Historical Beyond

i) The Temple Mount
    a) "Dome of the Rock," *The New Encyclopedia Britannica*, 1995 edition, vol. 4, p. 160.
    b) "Mohammed...AD570?–632," *Gage Canadian Dictionary*, (Ontario, Canada: Gage Publishing Limited, 1983) p.736.
    c) *Webster's Dictionary–1987 Edition* (section "M" in paperback) contains a more complete description: "Mo.hom.me. dan (mo.ham'.a. dan)
    a, of Mohammed or the Moslem religion; n.a Moslem. -ism n. Moslem religion; Islam [fr. Mohammed, Ar. Prophet, 570?–632]

    d) *Authorized King James Version*
    -Dan. 12:7, 11–12
    -Zech. 14:4

    e) The Gideon's International in Canada, 2006 Edition, 1997.
    -2 Thess. 2:3–4

ii) Heavens or Heaven?
    a) *Authorized King James Version*
    -Gen. 1:1–7
    -Gen. 2:1
    -Ps. 119:105

iii) Angels to Fallen Angels
    a) "In wine lies the truth."
    b) *Authorized King James Version*
    -Gen. 5:24,
    -Gen. 6:17,
    -Gen. 9:21
    -Prov. 20:1,

-Prov. 23:29–35
-Mark. 12:1–11
-Luke. 20:9–18
-John 2:1–11,
-John 4:7–42,
-John 8:3–11,
-John 11:1–2,
-John 12:3,
-John 19:25,
-John 20:1–18

iv) Great Primeval Flood
  a) *Mankind's Search for God* (NY: Watch Tower Bible and Tract Society of Pennsylvania, 1990). pp.46, 48–9.
  b) Ibid., ch.3 p. 46, par.9, "The Flood-Fact or Myth?"
  c) Ibid., ch.3 p. 46–48, par.10 "The Flood-Fact or Myth?"
  d) Ibid., ch.3, p. 48, par.12 "The Flood and the God-Man Gilgamesh."
  e) Ibid., ch.3, p. 48–49, par.13
  f) Ibid., ch.3, p. 49, par., 14
  g) Ibid., ch.3, p.49–52, par.15–19
  h) *Mankind's Search for God* (NY: Watch Tower Bible and Tract Society of Pennsylvania, 1990) pp.107, 116–7.
  i) Ibid., ch.5,b.p.107, a definition of the Hindi "Trimurti."
  j) Ibid., ch.5,t.p.116, "Brahma—the Creator God."
  k) Ibid., ch.5,b.p.117, "Siva."
  l) Ibid., ch.5,b.p.117, "Vishnu."
  m) *The Holy Bible—King James Version Bible Dictionary*, p.739.
  n) Parrinder, *G.,* "Primeval Flood," *The Routledge Dictionary of Religious and Spiritual Quotations* (London and New York: Taylor and Francis Group, 1990,2000) sec. no. 47, pp.b.53–54.

References

Armstrong, Herbert W., "The Separation of the Birthright. and the Sceptre," *The United States and Britain in Prophecy* (Worldwide Church of God, October 1984) ch.4, pp. 29–46.

Authorized King James Version with Explanatory Notes and Cross References to the Standard Works of the Church of Jesus Christ of Latter-Day Saints (Salt Lake City, UT: The Church of Jesus Christ of Latter-Day Saints, 1979).

Chamberlain, E. R., "II Diagnosis," *Jackdaw Fifty* (1973)

Chamberlain, E. R., "The Black Death," *Jackdaw Fifty* (1973)

"Constantine I—Roman Emperor," *The Encyclopedia Americana International Edition* (Danbury, CT: Grolier Educational, 2002) pp 7:647–9.

"Constantine I," *The World Book Encyclopedia* (Chicago, IL: World Book, Inc., 2006) CI: 993.

"Council of Nicaea," *The Encyclopedia Americana International Edition* (Danbury, CT: Grolier Educational, 2002) pp. 20:301.

"Dome of the Rock," *The New Encyclopedia Britannica*, 1995 edition, vol. 4, p. 160.

Findley, Mark A., *The Almost Forgotten Day* (Siloam Springs, AR: Concerned Group, Inc., 1988) pp.57, 60.

"Hitler," *The Encyclopedia Americana International Edition* (Danbury, CT: Grolier Educational, 2002) pp. 14:246–9.

"Hitler," *The World Book Encyclopedia* (Chicago, IL: World Book, Inc., 2006) H: 264–7.

Kane, Perry, "The Modern Age and the First Antichrist," *Nostradamus and the Millennium: What May Be Coming* (1999) b.p.19–t.p.20, p.21

Lindsey, Hal, *The Rapture: Truth or Consequences* (Bantam Book, August 1983) ch.2, pp.27–30; ch.12, pp.166–9.

Marcussen, Jan A., *National Sunday Law* (Thompsonville, IL: Amazing Truth Publications, 1983) pp.23–28; pp.91–92

Mankind's Search for God (NY: Watch Tower Bible and Tract Society of Pennsylvania, 1990). pp.46, 48–9; pp.107, 116–7.

Maxwell, Mervyn Ph.D., "The Message of Daniel for You and Your Family," *God Cares, Volume One* (Pacific Press Publishing Association, 1981) p.16.

Maxwell, Mervyn, Ph.D., "The Message of Revelation for You and Your Family," *God Cares, Volume Two* (Pacific Press Publishing Association, 1985) p.16.

"Mohammed…AD570?–632," *Gage Canadian Dictionary*, (Ontario, Canada: Gage Publishing Limited, 1983) p.736.

Gage Canadian Dictionary (p.736, paperback) contains a more complete, 3-part description of Mohammedan.

1) Mo. Ham.med (mo ham' id) n. A.D 570-632, a prophet and the founder of Islam, one of the world's great religions. His words are preserved in the Koran.

2) Mo.ham.med.an (mo ham' 2d2n) adj, n-adj. of or having to do with Mohammed or Islam. –n. Moslem."

3) Mo.ham.med. an. Ism (mo ham a dan iz am) n. Islam.

Mystery of the Ages (USA: Philadelphia Church of God, 1985, 2009) Second Edition, p. 122.

"Napoleon I," *The World Book Encyclopedia* (Chicago, IL: World Book, Inc., 2006) NI: 6–9.

"'Napoleon I," *The New World Family Encyclopedia* (New York, NY: Standard International Library, Inc., 1953) vol. 13, pp.3648–3651.

"Napoleon Bonaparte," *The Encyclopedia Americana International Edition* (Danbury, CT: Grolier Educational, 2002) pp. 19:728–33.

NAS New Testament with Psalms & Proverbs (The Lockman Foundation, 1997)

New American Standard Bible (The Lockman Foundation, 1995).

New World Translation of the Holy Scriptures (Brooklyn, NY: Watchtower Bible and Tract Society of New York, Inc., 1984; 1961, 1981, 1984).

"Nicene Councils," *The World Book Encyclopedia* (Chicago, IL: World Book, Inc., 2006) N: 402.

"Nostradamus," *The Encyclopedia Americana International Edition* (Danbury, CT: Grolier Educational, 2002) pp. 20:484.

"Nostradamus," *The World Book Encyclopedia* (Chicago, IL: World Book, Inc., 2006) N:550.

Orwell, George, "Oligarchical Collectivism," *1984* (Penguin Books, 1954) p.163.

Ovason, David, *Nostradamus—Prophecies for America* (New York, NY: Avon Books, 2001) pp.14, 63–9.

Parrinder, G., "Primeval Flood," *The Routledge Dictionary of Religious and Spiritual Quotations* (London and New York: Taylor and Francis Group, 1990, 2000) sec. no. 47, pp.b.53–54.

Pay Attention to Daniel's Prophecy (Brooklyn, NY: Watchtower Bible and Tract Society of New York, Inc., 1999) pp. 240.

Roberts, Henry, *The Complete Prophecies of Nostradamus* (Three Rivers Press, 1999) pp.63, 187, 292.

Smolley, Richard, "Century II, Quatrain 24," *The Essential Nostradamus* (New York, NY: Penguin Group (USA.) Inc., 2006) b.p.84–t.p.85.

The Book of Mormon: Another Testament of Jesus Christ (Salt Lake City, UT: The Church of Jesus Christ of Latter-day Saints, 1981)

"The Future of Religion and the Family," *Nostradamus for Dummies** (Indianapolis, IN: Wiley Publishing, Inc., 2005) p.280

The Gideon's International in Canada (Guelph, ON: Transcontinental Inc.) 2006 Edition.

The Holy Bible—King James Version Bible Dictionary, p.739.

The Holy Bible: Old and New Testaments in the Authorized King James Version (Stampley Enterprises, Inc., 1985).

"The Pearl of Great Price," *A Selection from the Revelations, Translations, and Narrations of Joseph Smith, First Prophet, Seer, and Revelator to the Church of Jesus Christ of Latter-Day Saints* (Salt Lake City, UT: The Church of Jesus Christ of Latter-Day Saints, 1981) Moses 5:26–28, "Cain and Abel"; Moses 7:69, "Zion Is Fled"; Moses 8:4, "A Great Famine."

These Times: The Amazing Prophecies of Daniel and Revelation (Hagerstown, MD: Review and Herald Publishing Association, 1983) pp.24–25.

Wigal, Donald Ph.D., *Visions of Nostradamus and Other Prophets* (Owings Mills, MD: Ottenheimer Publishers Inc., 1998) b.p.31–t.p.32; p.34.

About the Author

Various religious experiences of Harold G. Reynolds over the years have allowed him by God's providence to write and publish his first book. With much editing and rewriting over a ten-year period, *Vortex: Death Is Swallowed Up In Victory* is the book finally arrived at.

CPSIA information can be obtained
at www.ICGtesting.com
Printed in the USA
LVHW091757101118
596689LV00001B/1/P

9 781642 996043